Perseverance

Perseverance

The Story of Anne Sullivan Macy
(Helen Keller's Teacher)

Janice Larsen

To order additional copies of this book, contact:
Xlibris Corporation
1-888-795-4274
www.Xlibris.com
Orders@Xlibris.com
50749

Contents

Prologue 13

Chapter 1   1866, Feeding Hills, Massachusetts 15
Chapter 2   The Accident That Changed Our Lives, 1868-1870 21
Chapter 3   My New Friend Mary, 1872 27
Chapter 4   Disaster Strikes 30
Chapter 5   Goodbye, My Dear Mother 35
Chapter 6   More Moves, 1876 39
Chapter 7   About Tewksbury Almshouse 44
Chapter 8   Living at Tewksbury.. 47
Chapter 9   Jimmy 55
Chapter 10   Surgeries 58
Chapter 11   Back to Tewksbury.. 62
Chapter 12   History of Perkins School for the Blind.......... 67
Chapter 13   Life at Perkins... 70
Chapter 14   Laura Bridgman 77
Chapter 15   School and More Surgeries 79
Chapter 16   Tuscumbia, Alabama 83
Chapter 17   The Breakthrough.. 91
Chapter 18   Boston 97
Chapter 19   Desperation, 1892 103
Chapter 20   Looking for Schools 106
Chapter 21   Wright-Humason School................................. 110
Chapter 22   Cambridge, October, 1896............................... 113
Chapter 23   Radcliffe, 1900 116

Chapter 24 Wrentham, 1905-1913 120

Chapter 25 Lecture Circuit 126

Chapter 26 Hollywood and Vaudeville, 1918-1924 133

Chapter 27 Ireland, Scotland, and Brittany 137

Chapter 28 Last Light 143

Chapter 29 Farewell 145

Epilogue 147

To my granddaughter Shree
whose interest in Helen Keller led me to Anne Sullivan Macy

Special Thanks

Jan Seymour-Ford
for providing very helpful information from the
Perkins School for the Blind,
Watertown, Massachusetts.

————————

Virginia McClure
who encouraged me to write this book
and edited it for me.

————————

My son, Kirk,
who encouraged me all the way.

Author's Note

A few years ago I introduced my seven-year-old granddaughter Shree to the story of Helen Keller who as a result of "brain fever" had been blind and deaf since the age of nineteen months. Shree wanted to learn more, and I read several books and articles about Helen to provide this eager child with as much information as possible.

You can't read about Helen without Anne Sullivan. Anne was Helen's teacher, her eyes and her ears. She brought six-year-old Helen out of total darkness and taught this deafblind child to communicate. She accompanied her through school, and ultimately Helen graduated from Radcliffe College with a bachelor of arts degree. They were an inspiration to the world.

I was soon as interested in Anne as I was in Helen. I am amazed she overcame the terrible hardships of her youth to accomplish so much. Her early experiences, however, did leave scars. She suffered from depression, melancholy, anger, and distrust of people her entire life.

There is very little written about Anne. You find bits and pieces about her life in several books written about Helen, but a very limited number of books are dedicated to Anne herself.

It's hard to imagine how it must have felt to live Anne Sullivan's difficult life. In this book I try to express what her life must have felt like, through her eyes.

The events, places, and people in this book as well as Anne's disposition are fact based on the many books and articles I read and research on the Internet. The way Anne saw her world and the emotions she felt are what I imagine them to have been.

Prologue

January 17, 1935

I am an old woman now, and my days on this earth are numbered. My soul anxiously awaits the moment it is freed from the constraints of this old temple and returns to God, the One. However, before I leave, there is a story I must tell. It has been thirty years since Helen Keller wrote the story of her life, and she has pestered me for years to write my story. Even she, my companion for over half a century, does not know many of the events of my youth.

I have refused to tell my story before, going so far as to burn all of my diaries. I was ashamed and embarrassed and didn't want anyone to know about my childhood. I was convinced that my work would not be recognized or taken seriously if my past was known. Now, my frailness and blindness have dictated that I remain homebound, giving me a lot of time to look back over my life. And I realize that my story indeed must be told.

The experiences I had throughout my childhood were necessary to prepare me for what I was put on this earth to do. All of the people who reached out to me, even if just in passing, influenced the direction of my life. My experiences gave me the perseverance, knowledge, love, and understanding required to make the world accessible to an angry, uncontrollable blind and deaf child named Helen Keller. After coming out of complete darkness, she became an inspiration to people all over the world. As for me, I was able to experience the fun and wonder of my missed childhood through Helen: I saw the world and fulfilled my own passion for learning.

1

1866

FEEDING HILLS, MASSACHUSETTS

My father, Thomas Sullivan, was a handsome young man with dark hair, a devilish sense of humor, and a smile that endeared everyone to him. As was typical of most of the Irish immigrants, he was a common man who was illiterate and only qualified for hard labor. Mom, Alice Clohessy Sullivan, was a very pretty, energetic young woman with curly auburn hair and beautiful hazel eyes. They had recently made the long journey to America from Ireland on a ship I believe was called the *Mohongo,* which sailed from Derry to New York. They planned to join Dad's elder half brother John and brother J. H. Sullivan who both had arrived in America several years earlier and were settled into comfortable lives with their families as tobacco farmers in Feeding Hills, Massachusetts.

Feeding Hills was a sleepy little community in southern Massachusetts where many of the Irish immigrants settled to work on tobacco, dairy, or produce farms. Thousands of Irish people were coming to America to escape the poverty and hardships caused by the potato famine. Many times their trips were paid for by tobacco or dairy farmers in exchange for their labor.

It was bad timing for the Irish people's arrival in the United States. The Irish Fenians were stirring up trouble for the English and had just raided Quebec. Irish families were poor, and the disheartened, uneducated Irish men resorted to drinking and fighting. Most Americans resented the presence of the Irish because they were taking badly needed jobs and were perceived as no-goods and drunks. Twenty-three percent of the population of the area was Irish.

Rutherford B. Hayes was president of the United States, and the Civil War had recently ended. The Civil Rights Act had just passed, so I was automatically a U.S. citizen when I was born. During the previous administration of Ulysses S. Grant, the United States went into a serious depression. Unemployment was at an all-time high with people out of work fighting for the few jobs available. As a result, wages were low.

Mother was pregnant when they arrived in the United States. She and Dad were thrilled to be starting a family and were certain the future would bring them many healthy children and a much better life than they would have had in Ireland. Dad hoped to return to Ireland someday and use the money he earned in America to buy a farm there.

*   *   *

I was the first of five children born to Thomas Sullivan and Alice Clohessy. I made my appearance in a dilapidated old house called the Castle in Feeding Hills, Massachusetts, on April 12, 1866. The snow had recently melted, and everyone was eagerly watching for the rebirth of the trees when the buds opened their soft green leaves and the first signs of the wildflowers exhibited their beautiful array of color. Mother told me that the day I was born the sun rose to show off the brilliance of a beautiful spring day highlighting my welcome arrival. The long winter was over. My full name is Johanna Sullivan, but my dad insisted I be called Anne.

We shared the old three-story house with several other Irish families. It was far from being a castle. It was cold and drafty in the winter when the temperature dropped to as low as twenty degrees. In the summer it was hot and humid reaching a stifling ninety degrees.

The tenants of the house shared a putrid outside toilet in the backyard and during the hot humid summer the stench of it was unbearable. All of the water had to be carried in from a well next to the house. It was warmed in buckets on the wood stove for our baths and poured into a large tub placed in the center of the kitchen. Baths were taken about every two weeks. Everyone in the household used the same tub of water. The last person to use the bath, who was usually Mom, had cold dirty bath water with lye soap scum floating on top to bathe in.

The children all wore colorless old hand-me-down clothes shared between the families. Several times a year churches from the West

Springfield area brought welcome bags of used clothing and shoes to our community. It was like Christmas when our mother's searched through the clothing for outfits for their families.

The clotheslines sagged both winter and summer with rag diapers and faded, torn children's clothing. When it was freezing outside the women used the hallways to hang clothes. Otherwise the clothes hung outside would freeze into grotesque shapes and then would have to be dried again after they had thawed out. Dad assured Mother that we would soon have a nice home of our own. He detested living in the Castle.

*   *   *

My dear sister Nellie was born a year after my birth. We were still living in the Castle. She and I were always very close and when we were toddlers happily romped and played. We were seldom apart. As soon as we could crawl, we found we had lots of playmates living in the Castle. We loved racing around and hiding in the wet clothes when they were hung in the hallway, until one of the mothers would find their wet laundry all over the floor and shoo us away.

We didn't notice the lack of paint, loose floorboards, scarred doors, and dirty, broken windows of our home. It was our home. We knew nothing different. We had a wonderful big yard to play in with a large oak tree that shaded us lovingly as we played among the roots. The high grass and weeds made a wonderful hiding place for hide-and-seek. Mother played with us often and helped us find perfect sticks and stones to use as toys. I had several special stick dolls that I hid from the other children in the tall weeds or under the bed. Nellie and I loved to go next door with Mother to the cemetery and play. One of the monuments was shaped like a table, and we gathered sticks and stones and pretended to make a nice lunch for Mom.

The moms all watched over us, and we were treated to tasty treats when someone's father brought home a paycheck. Unfortunately, my dad seldom brought home a check. He was constantly being fired from jobs because of his drinking, hot temper, and absence from work. He would become distracted from the family, and there were long periods of time when he didn't come home at all. American life wasn't what he had expected. When he was absent, I sorely missed snuggling in his lap and listening to his stories. I felt so safe and warm when I curled up in his arms and leaned my head against his chest so I could hear his heartbeat and his soft, muffled voice when he talked to Mother as she cleared up the table.

I don't remember too much about our time at the Castle. I'm not sure what is my memory or what is remembered as a result of the stories

Mother and Dad told, but it seems that we were content most of the time and had lots of good times and many friends. My vague memories are of warmth and love.

*   *   *

The summer of 1868 when I was two years old and Nellie was one, my dad started working for John Taylor on his large farm. After goodbyes to all of our friends in the Castle and promises to see each other again soon, we moved to the farm down the street into a small cottage used for the hired hands. It was located across the road from the Taylors' home. Dad was quite excited to be giving his family their own home to live in.

The cottage consisted of a kitchen, living room, and two bedrooms. The floorboards were worn but clean. The walls had all been painted white and were stained from the smoke of the potbelly stove used to warm the kitchen and living room on cold winter days. Lots of windows let in welcome light. It looked as though many families had lived there before us. To us it was a mansion compared to our quarters at the Castle. And best of all Nellie and I had our own bedroom to share.

The fresh summer breeze brought the fragrance of the flowers, grass, and trees into our rooms where Mother would be mending, cleaning, or cooking us wonderful suppers from the fresh produce that was available on the farm.

The Taylors had chickens that would roam over into our yard for us to chase although we did have to avoid the mean old rooster. We visited a beautiful large brown-eyed black-and-white cow in the meadow regularly, but the pigs we were very strictly told to stay away from. We were thrilled when the cow we named Molly came to the fence and ate grass extended from our little hands. Molly provided us with delicious milk and cream, and we had fresh eggs from our chicken friends. Dad was happy again and walked with the air of a successful husband and father. Our little family was more contented than ever! Our first summer in our little cottage was wonderful.

To me, my mother was the most beautiful woman in the world. She had a wonderful voice and was always singing and teaching us Irish songs. She made us laugh. She played with us whenever she had a break from her household chores, and we never felt a lack of love or attention.

We always sat down to a nice supper as a family, and Mother did her best to be cheerful in spite of the fact that Dad occasionally went off drinking somewhere and probably wouldn't come home till the wee hours of the morning. When he did come home, he was boisterous and rough. On these nights, the three of us snuggled up in Mom's bed and listened to the crickets and night noises as we fell asleep. Then Mother carried each of us to our bed and waited for Dad to come home.

Over the years, Mother made every season of the year special even when she was sick. In spring we looked for wildflowers and put them in the middle of our kitchen table. They always made Mother cheerful, and we danced a dance for spring around the table.

In the summertime the family was often loaded into a borrowed horse-drawn wagon for trips to the Westfield River or travel the long eight miles to Congamond Lake to play in the water and have a picnic at Abell's picnic grounds.

Sometimes we went on these trips with our uncle John and his family. There were five children in Uncle John's family. Kate was a year older than me, and William was a year younger. They were perfect playmates for Nellie and me. Ellen, Daniel, and John were all a year apart; and John, the youngest of the three, was three years older than me.

All of the children were loaded into the back of the wagon to sit on bales of hay for our excursions. We were packed in the back with picnic baskets and old quilt blankets we used for our table.

At the river, beautiful cities were built in the mud, and sometimes we made delicious-looking mud cakes and cookies on the banks of the river. We had to watch Nellie closely because she always tried to eat the goodies we made.

I tried until my arms were sore to copy the older boys skipping rocks across the smooth surface of the river. Dad and Uncle John followed a path of rocks as far out into the river as possible to catch the fish lingering there for our dinner. No poles were necessary. They caught them with their hands.

When we went to the lake, castles rose out of the sand surrounded by moats with little stick bridges. Picnic lunches were especially good and made even better when Dad or our uncle told stories of Ireland. They told us about the kind, gentle faeries as well as wicked faeries, lucky flowers, and the creatures and plants that should be avoided. We sat wide-eyed hanging on every word.

Sometimes their stories were told in Gaelic that none of us understood, but we still sat quietly and listened. Every once in a while we were certain we saw a faerie dart off beside us, but we were assured that the faeries only existed in Ireland—unless of course one of them made its way into someone's pocket and hitchhiked a ride to America. We all checked our pockets looking for wayward faeries.

In the fall the hillsides were covered with the radiant color of the trees. We studied the veins of the brilliant gold and deep maroon leaves that had fallen behind our cottage, and we decorated every corner of our little home with them.

On Halloween my superstitious dad made sure we dressed up in costumes that made us look inhuman to scare away any demons that may have come over from the other world to steal us. On those nights he was especially careful to clean the hearth and set out a bowl of water for the faeries to bath their babies in and milk for them to drink to make certain we were in their favor. If salt was ever spilled, we always had to throw some over our left shoulder for luck, and Dad refused to ever cut down any blackberry bushes because he knew it would enrage the faeries.

In winter Mother excitedly took us outside to look at the first snowflakes of the year, even when she was sick. We tried catching them on our tongues and watched with wonder as they landed on our little hands. Mother told us they were each different and had their own design. I didn't tell her, but I never did see much difference between the flakes. Then we went inside, and Mother would fix us hot chocolate, and we made snowflakes out of old scraps of magazines.

If the weather permitted, Mother found every stitch of clothing in the house to bundle us in and let us play in the snow. We must have looked a sight! When it was too cold to go outside, or if Mother was sick, Nellie and I were perfectly content to play inside. Pans would be used for houses in a made-up village with cups for wagons and spoons or clothespins for people. We had no toys and had no idea we were poor.

These few fond memories that my mother and dad shared with me and the ones I remember have been a treasure to me my entire life. On the rare occasions that I allow myself to think about my childhood, I force myself to think of these happy places and times because it wasn't much later that my life changed drastically and our lives became quite dreary.

2

1868-1870

THE ACCIDENT THAT CHANGED OUR LIVES

In October 1868, Mother was huge with the weight of the baby she was carrying. She was having a great deal of trouble getting around and had me help her as much as a two-year-old was able. In addition, she had a cold that she couldn't get rid of and coughed much the time. She was very tired.

One crisp fall morning after Dad had gone to work, Mother thought it would be a perfect time to wash the floorboards before she was too big to be able to get down on the floor. They would dry quickly with the warm autumn breeze blowing through the door. Mother got a large bucket of water from the pump, a brush, and lye soap; shooed us out of the house to gather fall leaves in the yard; and began mopping the floor on her hands and knees.

When she stood up to get a fresh bucket of water, she lost her balance and fell against the potbelly stove. We heard a terrible crash and her heart-wrenching scream of pain. I ran into the house and saw that the stove had fallen on her, and her legs were pinned under it. Nellie screamed in horror in the background as I tried desperately to help Mother move the stove, but we just didn't have the strength to move it.

There was no one else around, and Mother told me to run and get my dad who was working in one of the tobacco fields on the Taylor farm across the road. I ran as fast as I could across to the farm screaming his name as loudly as my breathless lungs could muster. Dad finally heard me and came running. I told him Mother had fallen and couldn't get up and the stove was on her legs.

Dad rushed home, and by the time I got there, he had lifted the stove off her legs and carried her to the couch. Sobbing and with tears streaming down my face, I helped Dad get cool wet towels and wrap them around her legs. Blinking away my tears, I saw her legs were swollen and red with deep red marks where the stove had pressed against them. Her feet looked purple. In vain, she tried to hide her pain from Nellie and me. It was very frightening to see her struggle and choke back her moans and tears.

I didn't leave her side for the next several days and soothed and nursed her as best I could by rubbing her arms and giving her cold wet cloths to put on her legs. I insisted on doing everything for her. Then after what seemed an eternity, Mother managed to get out of bed and attempt her household chores. I was so frightened and sad to see her try to walk. I vividly remember my beautiful, vivacious mother grimacing in pain while she struggled to walk across the room using the walls, chairs, and table to lean on. I bravely ran to help her, but I was too little to be of much assistance. Mother praised me anyway for all my help and told me she didn't know what she would do without me. After the accident, she wasn't able to play with us much anymore, and we were shooed outside as often as the weather permitted while she rested. Her legs would never heal properly, and she had trouble walking for the rest of her life.

By winter, Mom's stomach had grown much larger; and when she wasn't sitting with her feet propped up, she hobbled around the house on crutches. Before Dad left for work, he made sure there was plenty of wood by the stove so Mother could easily keep us warm.

Through all of this pain and suffering, she continued to lavish love and attention on Nellie and me. We cuddled up next to her, and she told us stories about Ireland and sang her favorite Irish songs. She reminded us of the fun things we did over the summer and fall and the adventures we had while we lived in the Castle.

Sometimes we played guessing games and imagined what we were going to be when we grew up. Mother always had Nellie and me dressed in beautiful lacy dresses and carried off in large colorful carriages sitting beside rich farmers who were to become our husbands. She always had strong large white horses pulling our shiny carriages. The back of the carriages held large trunks filled with our beautiful clothes and shoes. We would live in mansions and have beautiful, healthy children and lots of friends. We'd throw lavish parties with wonderful things to eat. We talked about how we would decorate our homes. Our pretend homes were always filled with toys and sweets; and we both had lots of dogs, horses, and other animals.

Dad came home from work every day very tired but happy to see his precious family. He didn't leave home for extended periods of time or come home drunk as often as he had before Mother had her accident. He was very attentive to Mother and worried over her painful legs and cough.

In the evening the whole family curled up on Mother and Dad's bed and listened to Dad's stories. I usually sat right next to Mother with my hand on her large belly feeling my sibling kick.

*   *   *

It was a snowy cold evening in January 1869 when Mother started complaining of stomach pain. Dad hurried out and walked through the deep snow to our neighbor's house for help. By the time Dad and Mrs. Fitzgerald came back, Mother was in agony. Nellie and I sat in a corner of the room terrified at what was happening to our mom. Dad grabbed Nellie and me up in his arms and took us to our bed assuring us everything was fine.

Fear and confusion kept us awake for what seemed like hours until we were exhausted and fell asleep in each other's arms. I was awakened later to hear my mother screaming. I lay petrified and shaking, wondering what could be happening to my mom. I couldn't move. All of a sudden the screaming stopped. All I could hear was whispering and then a faint cry. I was sitting up in my bed when Dad came in and told me I had a little brother. His name was Jimmy. It was very difficult for me to go back to sleep, but in time I did.

The next morning I had my first glimpse of my beloved little Jimmy. He was very tiny with a little round face and red hair. When I, with Mom's help, carefully examined his little fingers, toes, arms, and legs, I discovered a large lump or bunch on his leg. Dad and Mother assured me he would be fine, and we all tried to resume our normal lives.

However, Mother didn't recover quickly from the birth of Jimmy. Her coughing worsened, and she grew very thin and weak. The lump on Jimmy's leg did not go away. He cried if his leg was touched or bumped and slept fretfully. Mother was unable to do much of anything around the house except cook our supper and take care of Jimmy.

Several nights a week, Mom's good friend Catherine Fitzgerald brought us our supper. I was responsible to watch over Nellie, and when Mother was cooking, I watched over little Jimmy. I got the clean diapers for Jimmy, kept Nellie out of trouble, and fetched things for Mother when she needed them.

She couldn't walk without a great deal of pain or bend over and pick anything up off the floor, and she would have frightening coughing fits that left her red faced and gasping for air. Nellie and I crawled under our bed or hid behind furniture when this happened until the coughing subsided. Usually these attacks would frighten Jimmy, and it would take what seemed like hours to calm him down. I was horrified when I saw blood coming from Mom's mouth after one of these coughing spells.

As the cold winter continued, the closed-up house stank from the dirty diapers and dirty clothes lying about. The floors were filthy. Dirty dishes were piled in the sink, and our bed linens hadn't been cleaned for weeks and smelled of dirt and urine.

Each morning Nellie and I looked through the few ragged hand-me-down dresses we had which were either too small or too large and very dirty and dress ourselves as best we could. We hadn't taken a bath for weeks.

When I complained about the smell to Mother, she asked me to take the diapers and dirty clothes out in the backyard. I didn't want to touch any of them. I realized however that I was the only one there who could perform this horrible task. I grabbed an armful and ran out the back door and threw them next to the outhouse!

Dad started coming home late again, and many times he had spent his badly needed wages on drinking. He was still very tender with Mother and Jimmy when he was home but quickly lost patience with Nellie and me when we played noisily or nagged him to play with us or tell us stories like he used to. Then one day he was brought home in a wagon with a serious wound to his leg caused from an accident with a scythe used while cutting tobacco. He was housebound for several days, which made him depressed and angry. I made certain I stayed well out of his reach.

As the seasons came and went that year, Mother struggled to get up and feed us. However, she continued our celebrations of every season even though she couldn't really participate. She sat outside on a chair holding Jimmy and encouraged our spring and summer wildflower and butterfly hunts. In the fall she savored the beauty of the trees from the doorstep while we romped in the dead leaves. We bundled ourselves up under Mom's supervision for winter outings in the yard, and she and Jimmy watched us from a frosty window.

*   *   *

Beautiful spring finally came with the tree buds opening to worship the sun and the wildflowers popping their heads up everywhere. It was time to play outside! How fresh the air smelled after being cooped up all winter in the filthy house. Mother wasn't feeling any better, and I welcomed the time I could spend outside of that dreary house. I was three, and Nellie was two, so we were old enough to play outside by ourselves.

It was my responsibility to watch over Nellie. She was a beautiful little girl with reddish brown hair, light complexion, and a beautiful smile. Everyone who saw her adored her. I wasn't a pretty child. My face was too round, and my hair tended to get frizzy. I did not smile as much as Nellie and had a permanent turning down of my lips that made me appear as though I were pouting all the time. Jimmy was adorable in spite of the pain he was in from his leg. His hair was the same color as Nellie's and was very curly. His eyes glistened. When he laughed, we all had to laugh. He was so tiny and frail though, and it seemed he would never grow.

*   *   *

There was a big old apple tree in the corner of our yard that I was especially fond of. It was old and gnarly with strong, sturdy branches that had withstood many Massachusetts storms. It had a low branch that allowed me to crawl up into its leafy arms and feel the loving, protective energy of its being surround me. To my delight, Nellie was too little to climb the tree, so it was my own private haven.

I spent many an hour sitting quietly with pretend faeries in that tree. The faeries were beautiful little creatures that told me magical stories and listened so well to all of mine. My favorite faerie to which I talked the most was named Lily.

As an adult, I always thought about faerie friends when I walked in the woods or saw a beautiful big tree. Little did Dad know that there were actually faeries in America! They had to have followed us to America because they spoke to me with an Irish brogue.

I believe that tree was the beginning of my lifelong love of trees. The out-of-doors was my refuge, the tree my loving strong home, the faeries my healthy loving family, the green grass a clean colorful floor, and the flowers my friends nodding their beautiful little heads as I passed by.

Many times I took refuge in my tree to talk to the faeries, especially about Jimmy and Mom. The lump on Jimmy's leg had grown larger, and at the age of a year and a half, he could not walk. I loved him so much and wanted him to be able to run and play with us. Mother was coughing more and more and could do very little without having to stop and lie down.

Fortunately Mrs. Fitzgerald brought our supper several nights a week or I'm afraid we would have had to just eat raw vegetables from the garden. We had plenty of food from the farm, but Mother couldn't stand long enough to prepare it. Dad was not coming home very much again, and when he did, I stayed far away from him. He was always angry with me.

*   *   *

When I was four years old, Mother started vomiting again, and her stomach grew. Soon we all knew that she was going to have another baby. Mother was resting on the bed one day with Jimmy when it was time for the bread to come out of the oven. She called to me and asked me to take it out of the oven. I was afraid I would get burned, so I said no! Mother convinced me I could do it, but in the end I did get burned and dropped the bread on the floor. I was so angry that I stomped on the bread and then took the other loaf out of the oven and stomped on it as well.

All of the anger and fear I had hidden deep within over the last few years exploded in an outburst of horrible rage. As soon as Dad found out what I had done, he whipped me soundly! I know I deserved it, but I was so miserable and angry living in that house with Mother sick and the stink of the place I deeply resented him punishing me. I hated him at that moment, and that hatred grew as the years passed.

Many more whippings followed as a result of my bad behavior. I could no longer control myself. Dad watched me constantly looking for me to do something wrong, which I invariably did just because I hated him so. The more I got whipped, the more I hated him and the worse my behavior became.

Mother gave birth to Mary in the fall of 1871. She was a healthy, contented bright-eyed baby who brought a welcome diversion to our struggling family.

3

1872

MY NEW FRIEND MARY

I turned six in April 1872. Things hadn't changed at home. Mother was still coughing and unable to walk well, and Jimmy's leg was no better. The lump on his leg seemed larger. He was three years old, very small and frail looking and could only hobble around with a cane.

As much of my time as possible was spent outside because it was filthy dirty in the house. I loved my siblings, but I was tired of having to take care of them. As I sat in my tree early one morning, I saw a girl from the Taylor farm across the street walk up the road with beautiful clothes on, carrying a package and books. I rushed outside early every morning to see her walk by. Finally after several days of seeing this young girl, I got up the courage to run out to the roadside and talk to her. She told me her name was Mary Taylor and that her father had died, and they had come to live with her aunt Eliza who owned the farm.

Eliza's husband, John Taylor, died just a few years earlier; and she was happy to have her sister-in-law and niece there to help her and keep her company. Her son John E. Taylor lived and worked the farm for her; but he drank too much, had a short temper, and would disappear for days.

The hired help despised him, and it fell on Eliza's shoulders to direct the activities of the farm.

I asked Mary where she was going, and she told me she was going to school. "What's school?" I asked, and she proceeded to tell me the wonderful things they did at school. I asked her if I could go with her, but she said I'd have to wait until the next school term that started in the fall. She suggested I go to school with her to visit sometime.

Of course I was elated, and after asking my mother, I soon found myself getting ready for my school visit! Mother managed to wash my best dress and found a pair of decent shoes to cover my feet. I took a much-needed bath and washed my hair as best I could. The shoes hurt my feet something awful, but I didn't object because Mother insisted I have shoes on to go to school.

The school was a typical one-room brick schoolhouse with the teacher's desk in the front of the room next to the blackboard, a potbelly stove in the corner of the room, and the children's benches and tables spread across the middle of the room facing the blackboard. There was another little room called the cloak closet where the children hung their coats and put their lunch packages.

There was an outhouse in the back and a swing hanging from a gigantic tree on the playground. A pump was near the back door with a string attaching a large ladle that we all drank from to quench our thirst. A bucket caught the spilled water, and we used that water with lye soap to wash our hands before going back into the classroom.

The teacher was very nice and very pretty. She introduced me to the class and asked each child to stand and tell me their names. I was so excited to be in this magnificent place. I know I had a huge smile on my face as I slipped beside Mary into her assigned bench seat. I was given a used slate board and slate pencil and told to copy what was on the board. Paper, pencils, and ink were available but only used occasionally.

The desktops were worn and scratched, and you could tell where the children placed their bottles of ink from the circle of ink at each place. The room smelled of chalk and books and lunches and smoke from the fires that had burned in the stove. I took my time carefully copying everything exactly as it was on the blackboard even though I had no idea what the lines and loops meant.

Soon it was recess, and the girls invited me to play jump rope and cat's cradle with them. The boys ran races and had contests to see who could run the fastest or who could spit or throw stones the farthest. After recess, Mary shared her reader with me, and I pretended I was able to follow along as Miss Summers had the children each take a turn reading. Thankfully she didn't call on me.

The children worked on spelling, reading, writing, and arithmetic. They learned rhymes to memorize their multiplication tables. At lunchtime we all sat under a big elm tree and ate lunches packed either in parcels of paper or in small buckets.

When we returned to class, the teacher showed us a colorful large map of the United States. As she pointed a stick at each different colored shape, the children raised their hands eager to be called upon to name the state. A globe of the entire world sat on a stand in the corner. I didn't understand much of anything the children were learning, but it was the most exciting day of my life. I vowed to myself that I would go to school and learn everything there was to learn.

*   *   *

Whenever I could get away from my babysitting responsibilities, I spent many wonderful hours with my new friend Mary. She was ten years older than me and had a great deal to teach me. We spent sunny afternoons nestled under a tree while she read me stories from beautiful books about places all over the world. Some of the books had pictures of faraway places. When the weather was such that we couldn't play outside, we played in her house. It was a large two-story wood-frame house with several bedrooms on the second floor. In her bedroom, she had her very own desk and two beautiful dolls to play with. The dolls even had different dresses they could wear. I never had a doll.

We explored the garden, and she taught me about the different flowers and bugs that lived there. She laughed when I stuck up my nose after I smelled the trillium wildflower that is also called Stinking Willie.

We gathered sunflowers, bloodroot, and wild geraniums that I proudly presented to my dear mom. I learned about caterpillars and butterflies. Mary taught me numbers, and I learned to count to one hundred.

This time with Mary was my only real happiness during that period of my life. When I was with her, I forgot about the problems at home. She gave me hope. I could go to school like her! I could learn to read!

4

DISASTER STRIKES

With the arrival of summer, my sister Nellie came down with a fever, Mother was getting weaker and weaker, and Jimmy's hip was swelling more, giving him a lot of pain. It made me so sad to see him cry with pain when he tried to play. The house was a mess, and with the summer heat, the stench from the dirty clothes and diapers all over the floor made it nearly unlivable. It didn't even help clear the stench when all of the doors and windows were open to let in a breeze.

Mother spent most of her time in a chair in the living room. Nellie was in our bed, and it was impossible for Mother to constantly get up and take care of her. So I assumed much of the responsibility.

Several times when I felt Nellie's head, she was very hot, and she wouldn't even drink water. I put cold wet cloths on her head as Mother directed, and she would get a little bit better.

One dreadful morning that summer, I woke up and couldn't open my eyes. It was like they were taped shut. Mother wiped my eyes with a wet cloth, and when I opened them, they were sore and red. Mother started boiling geranium leaves and putting drops of the liquid in my eyes.

Several weeks passed, and they were no better. I could hardly see. When I was outdoors, I could see the outline of objects and color; but in the house where it was darker, I couldn't see very much of anything.

When I went across the street to see Mary, I was told I needed to go home and was not allowed to see her anymore because her mother was afraid she'd catch what I had. It made me so angry that I had to stay inside that filthy house and not play outside or ever see Mary. I would scream, knock over anything in my path, and pound my fists on the walls and bed. I hated everything and everyone.

I constantly got whippings from Dad. To make matters worse, when I asked Mother how many days it was until I went to school, she told me I couldn't go because I couldn't see well enough. My only hope was that my eyes would get better.

A few weeks later, Dad told me he was going to take me into the town of Westfield with him to see a doctor about my eyes. I was elated and jumped up and down with joy knowing that I would soon see and be able to go to school.

*   *   *

As we drove to Westfield, I used all of my other senses to experience the new surroundings around me. I smelled the flowers and trees, the dusty streets of the town, and the manure; heard the chatter of people walking the streets, the clatter of horses' hoofs, and occasionally got a whiff of something wonderful cooking. I squinted and shielded my eyes from the sun in an effort to see the outlines of the buildings of the town.

The doctor's office was upstairs above the general store. I was led into a clean little room and sat up on a high table for him to look at my eyes. I screamed in pain when he pulled the lids of my eyes up.

The news from Dr. Holland was devastating. We were told that there was nothing he could do. I had a condition known as trachoma, a contagious inflammation of the mucous membrane of the eyeball and eyelids, caused by bacterial infection. It sometimes causes blindness.

All the way home I cried like I had never cried before. Hope was gone. I could not control my tears even with the comforting hand of my dad on my back. I knew then that I would not be able to go to school. I vowed determinedly to myself that someday, somehow I'd learn to read.

*   *   *

It was a very cold winter, and once again my time was spent in the filthy, stinking house. But what made it worse is that I didn't have Nellie to play with. She was over her fever but couldn't talk or get out of bed. Jimmy played a little, but since he couldn't move about without a great deal of pain, there wasn't much we could play. I helped him as best I could, but if I would by accident touch his hip, he would cry out in pain and anger.

Mary was a year old, and since Mother was still sick, it was my responsibility at the age of six to take care of her. I could hardly see, was clumsy, and dropped things. Mary was getting too heavy for me to carry. I was less and less patient with Jimmy and sassed Mother and Dad regularly causing me to get more and more whippings from Dad.

I hated my life. I hated being told to feed Mary, give Jimmy something to eat, change Mary's diaper, take out the dirty diapers, and help with meals. I became more and more insolent and withdrawn. I was a very ugly, hateful little girl.

*   *   *

In April I turned seven, and spring finally came. I went outside as much as possible to get away from the stench of the house and all of my responsibilities. However, since I couldn't see well, I had to find other ways to enjoy the beauty of spring and the freedom it brought with it. I climbed my tree and was delighted that the faeries were still there to talk to me and soothe my concerns. They understood.

I taught myself to find the wildflowers Mary had shown me by using my sense of smell. My fingers showed me their shapes, and I would remember their vivid bright colors. The feel of a butterfly breezing by my face filled me with awe, and I filled my lungs with the freshness of the season. I could smell the rain before it came. I followed the buzz of bees to the sunflowers and Queen Ann's lace. Dragonflies flew past me to announce their arrival and say hello. I recognized the bird's calls and pictured them in my mind. I learned to see without my eyes. Oh, how I loved the spring!

*   *   *

My ecstasy was short lived. In May my best friend and beloved sister Nellie died. She had been sleeping for several weeks. One morning when I went in to see her, I touched her face, and it was cold. Dad came in and told me Nellie had died and wouldn't be sick anymore. She was in heaven now where she could play and sing with other children. She wasn't cold and had beautiful clothes to wear. She had lots of good things to eat. When I left the room, I wished I had been able to go with her. She would be able to go to school, and I couldn't.

Dad and I took Nellie's casket to the cemetery. Mother was pregnant again and not feeling well, and someone had to stay home with Jimmy and Mary. The priest was waiting for us at the Calvary Cemetery in Chicopee.

Dad and I were the only other ones there besides the priest. Hand in hand we watched them lower her little casket into the grave. A few words from the priest and it was over. I didn't want to leave her.

Dad held my hand, and for several minutes we stood by the grave and wept together. There are no words to express the pain and agony I felt that day. How could the sun still shine and birds still sing when my sister Nellie was dead? The world should have stopped. I still weep for Nellie.

* * *

The following month on the same date Mary was born, Mother gave birth to Johnny. He was a frail baby and cried all of the time. He was unable to nurse. Thankfully it was warm enough for Jimmy, Mary, and me to spend most of our days outside; so we didn't have to hear him cry. Oh, how I missed Nellie.

Jimmy, Mary, and I were outside playing in the dirt when I suddenly realized that it was very quiet in the house. I was happy that Johnny finally stopped crying.

When I went inside, Mother was washing Johnny at the table. His tiny body was perfectly still. Mother was crying and said he had died and wasn't hungry anymore. He was with Nellie. She put him in his best nightdress and wrapped him in a blanket.

The next day we all went to the cemetery and buried little Johnny right next to my beloved Nellie. I felt very guilty that I didn't feel the least bit bad that Johnny had died. All during the service for him, I just looked at Nellie's grave. I shed no tears. It was a relief to me that it would be quiet in the house again.

I thought a lot about death after that day. Exactly where were Nellie and Johnny? Was Nellie in school? Was Johnny a happy fat baby? How could that be when we put their bodies into the ground?

* * *

I was very lonesome. I was not allowed to get near my friend Mary Taylor anymore because her mother was afraid she would catch the disease I had in my eyes. I was not allowed to even cross the street and go into her yard.

Mary's cousin John and his wife, who also lived there, had just had a new baby; and I noticed it was outside by the house in its buggy. No one else was out there, so I decided I'd just sneak over and take a peek at the baby. Just as I was lifting the mesh covering the buggy, John caught me and yelled, "Get away from that baby, you filthy Irish brat!"

Dad heard the commotion and was by my side immediately. For the first time in my life, my dad defended me. He yelled at me to go home, and as I was running home, I turned around and saw Dad and John fighting. I ran into the house and told Mother what had happened. We both knew I was in a lot of trouble, and she grabbed me and pushed me under the bed.

Dad came staggering into the house with blood all over the front of his shirt. Mother rushed to see if he was all right, but he brushed her away and told her it wasn't his blood but the blood of John.

He yelled for me to come to him, but I stayed huddled in my hiding place. He knew where I was and pulled me out from under the bed and began yelling and beating me because I had caused him to lose his job.

*   *   *

A week or so later, we moved into two rooms on the second floor of a boardinghouse in Feeding Hills. I loved the boardinghouse. There were giant trees in the yard, and it had a large porch that extended across the front of the house. I could hear children playing in the schoolyard down the street. I squinted and shaded my eyes in an attempt to see the little white schoolhouse, but all I saw was a blur. Once I wandered down to the schoolhouse, but when the teacher saw me, she took one look at my eyes and told me not to come back.

Dad soon found another job on a tobacco farm. I stayed far away from him. We had taken a step backward because of me. We had lost our little cottage home and were back in a house living with other families again.

5

GOODBYE, MY DEAR MOTHER

On January 19, 1874, my mother died of tuberculosis. I remember kissing her good night and getting a hug and kiss in return, and then the next morning she was dead. In one year I had lost my best friend and sister Nellie, my newborn brother Johnny, and now the biggest loss of all, my mom. Dad tearfully told me that she was now with Nellie and Johnny. Where? Why, oh why, couldn't I have gone with her? What would I do now?

Jimmy, Mary, and I only had each other. I had to be the mother, and I was only eight years old. Who would protect me from Dad? Our rooms in the boardinghouse immediately were cold and quiet. Something dreadful had happened, and the power of my mom's love was no longer there for us. I felt very much alone.

Dad had no money, so Mother was buried in potter's field with the help of donations from our neighbors. There was just a graveyard service. Mother had lots of friends from the Castle who came. Everyone was very kind to us. After the service everyone went back to the boardinghouse and ate the food our friends had brought. We had enough food to last for several days. I ate nothing and spent the day sitting alone on the back porch. I could not bear to hear any more stories or talk about my mom.

*   *   *

After Mom's death, Dad was drunk all the time and lost his job again. During the long days he lay in bed, loudly snoring a drunkard's snore and when awake wailing and crying. He was certain that he had been cursed for leaving his parents in Ireland. He blamed the landlords for everything that had happened to us in America. At night he went out drinking.

Jimmy, Mary, and I tried to stay out of his way and played quietly in another room. Jimmy suffered a great deal from Mom's death and hung on me until I had to beg him to leave me alone. Mrs. Fitzgerald and our cousin Ellen Sullivan came every day and brought us things to eat. Cousin Ellen usually brought her sewing and stayed with us for the entire day. They took our dirty clothes home and washed them and made sure we were bathed and clean. However, they soon lost their patience with Dad and insisted he go find a job and take care of his children.

Dad finally sobered up and got another job on a farm. Cousin Ellen continued coming to stay with us in the daytime. I was expected to carry a lunch to Dad every day. I enjoyed taking him his lunch because it gave me time to myself to enjoy the out-of-doors. My eyes were painful, and my vision was very blurry, but I could see well enough to walk to the farm where he worked. Since I could barely see, I used all my other senses to enjoy my walks.

In the spring and summer, I could smell the flowers, hear the birds and bees, and feel the breeze across my face and blowing through my hair. In the fall, I listened to the crackle of the dried leaves as I walked through them and picked up the newly fallen leaves to feel the fine veins that ran through their velvet bodies. How I missed seeing clearly their vivid colors.

Winter was quiet. When I took Dad his lunch, the only sound I heard was my feet breaking the surface of the crusty snow. It was so quiet my ears almost hurt with listening. Sometimes I heard a train whistle off in the distance and daydreamed about where it was going.

I had to pass the little white schoolhouse on each of these trips. Sometimes I'd sneak up and stand outside a window in an effort to hear the sounds of the school day. I didn't do this too often because it made me sad, and I would stand and sob with desire to attend school. I was very lonely and wanted so badly to be one of the children in that schoolhouse.

People saw me and avoided me because of my eyes and my angry, sullen disposition. They would not let their children play with me. I wanted to play again without worrying about Jimmy and Mary; and I wanted so badly to learn reading, spelling, and writing.

*   *   *

Another fall and winter was approaching when Uncle John Sullivan told Dad he didn't think he was able to take care of us any longer. Dad was behind on the rent at the boardinghouse and unable to feed and clothe us properly.

Uncle John said his daughter Ellen could not come and sit with us every day anymore. He offered to take Mary and Jimmy to his small home, and Dad and I could stay in a recently abandoned one-room schoolhouse on his property. I was nine years old.

The schoolhouse had a stove and room for two cots. Uncle John said his wife, Mary, would send us our meals. He told me I could come and visit whenever I liked. Also, Aunt Mary could probably use my help with Jimmy and Mary. Why didn't they want me? Why couldn't I go and stay in the nice, warm house and play with the children? I didn't want to stay alone with Dad. I knew it was because I was an ugly, difficult child, and they were afraid of my diseased eyes.

Now I would lose Jimmy and Mary as my daily companions and would be alone during the cold winter months when the weather made walking to Uncle John's house to play with them impossible.

As often as I could, I trudged up the hill and through a field to Uncle John's home to take care of Jimmy and Mary and, when there was time, to play with my cousins. Uncle John and Aunt Mary had five children at the time ranging in age from eight to fourteen. William was eight and my favorite. I loved following him around when he did his chores. We played many happy hours in the barn or played games on rainy cold days in their warm house after chores were completed. I waited eagerly for them to come home from school and tell me about their school day. I wanted so badly to be able to go to school with them!

Aunt Mary made me take care of Jimmy and Mary, help clean house, and prepare meals. She made me wash my hands several times a day with lye soap to keep her children from being infected by me. My hands were red and raw. I knew she got frustrated with me when I couldn't do my chores well because of my lack of sight, but she refrained from scolding me.

At the end of the day, I trudged home with our supper in hand. Dad was never home during the day and many nights didn't come home at all. I ate my supper alone after which I curled up on my cot and told myself stories until I fell asleep. It was difficult for me to fall asleep at night. It was very dark, and the night noises were sometimes frightening.

When the wind blew or it was storming, I was especially scared. During those times, I would loudly sing the Irish songs my mother taught me. I

pretended Mother and Nellie were there singing with me. I strained my
ears and listened for Mom's laughter, and when I was certain I felt her
presence, I fell into a peaceful sleep.

*   *   *

I overheard Uncle John tell Aunt Mary that Dad wasn't working
again. My heart sunk. I was afraid if Dad wasn't working, he might come
home during the day. Even though I was a little frightened to stay in the
schoolhouse at night by myself, I was glad when Dad was not there. He was
always hitting me. When he finally did come home, he woke me up with
his noisy, drunken stumbling and cursing. On those nights I hurried and
wrapped myself in a blanket and scurried under my cot lying close to the
wall so he would think I wasn't there.

At times my eyesight was especially bad. Bright light made them hurt,
and I could see next to nothing in the dark. When I blinked, it felt like my
eyelids were made of sand.

6

1876

MORE MOVES

It was cold and windy the morning my uncle J. H. Sullivan knocked on the door. I was alone at the time. I didn't know JH because our families never got together. There obviously had been a rift between him and my dad. He told me that I was going to go and live with him; his wife, Anastasia; daughter Anna, who was one-year-old; and his sister Bridget. When I asked him about Jimmy and Mary, he told me they were going to stay at Uncle John's; and I could walk down the road and visit them occasionally, though I never did.

My aunt Anastasia, whom I was told to call Cousin Stasia, was very strict and obviously not very happy I had come to live with them. She demanded that I stay away from the baby. I slept across the foot of Uncle JH and Cousin Stasia's bed.

Uncle JH was a very kind man, but he never showed me any affection. I was fed and clothed, but that was about it. I was so envious when he held his daughter Anna on his lap and sang to her. It brought back faint memories of my earlier childhood when Dad cuddled me, told me stories, and sang his Irish songs.

I sat quietly in the back of the room and watched this happy little family's exchanges of love pretending that I was Anna. Aunt Bridget was kind enough to me but was afraid to get too close to me in case she caught my eye disease. No one wanted to get near me. How I longed for hugs from my mother and dad.

I did have a good friend though. His name was Rex, a lovable large mongrel dog. He seemed to sense my loneliness and always greeted me with lots of sloppy, wet kisses. His tail wagged his entire back end when he saw me.

Rex followed closely on my heels on all my excursions on the farm. When I tripped over a branch or rock that I couldn't see, he raced to my side, nudging me in an attempt to help me up.

Rex was the only one, besides the faeries, that ever saw me cry while I was living there. What a good friend he was. Rex, the birds, squirrels, and other creatures on the farm were my closest family. The chickens greeted me with joy when I brought table scraps out to their pen for their breakfast and happily let me retrieve their eggs from the nests. Nellie, the cow's, big black eyes always welcomed me when I visited during milking time. She stood patiently as I kissed and hugged her. As an adult, I was never without a dog or two and would have loved to have a farm full of animals.

It was mid-December, and Cousin Stasia and Aunt Bridget were decorating for Christmas. Lots of homemade ornaments were hung all over the beautiful big tree that JH had cut from the woods behind the house. I was given the job to weave popcorn on a long string to ultimately be draped around the tree. I believe I ate as much as I strung, but nobody seemed to mind.

I helped prepare for the festivities as much as my sight would allow. Everyone was in high spirits; and I remember how pleasant it felt in the nice, warm house, the tree decorated beautifully, and the smell of cookies and other sweets baking.

I was given strict orders to stay out of the front bedroom. Of course that just made me curious. So when no one was around, I snuck into the bedroom. There on the bed was the most beautiful doll in the world. I had never had a new toy and was certain this doll was mine. I returned to the bedroom as many times as possible and held that doll. I named her Dolly.

On Christmas morning, everyone rushed to the Christmas tree to open presents. I was handed a couple of small packages containing hankies and a ribbon for my hair and a pretty comb-and-brush set. Then at last Cousin Stasia reached down and picked up the box with Dolly in it. My heart was racing I was so excited.

She opened it and showed us the doll, and then she walked over and gave it to Anna. I couldn't believe it. Dolly was not mine! I started screaming and crying that Dolly was mine, and finally Uncle JH pulled me from the room to the back of the house where I was left for the remainder of the festivities.

That was a disappointment I remembered with bitterness my entire life.

*   *   *

The remainder of the winter I spent as much time as possible out-of-doors with Rex, in the barn and when necessary in the house. I didn't see Jimmy or Mary all winter. After the Christmas fiasco, Cousin Stasia ignored me except when she asked me to do something. I couldn't help around the house anymore because of my eyesight, and I was obviously a burden to them. I was left on my own most of the time. Thank goodness for Rex. He was a wonderful, loving companion to me.

In the welcome spring and summer, Rex and I spent all of our time exploring the farm and the fields. I found a huge oak tree under which I sat and became acquainted with the many birds that lived amongst its richly leafed branches. If I sat still enough, one bird in particular would come and sit on my hand.

Lily and the other faeries also kept me company. They joined me at the brook where I made all kinds of things out of mud. It brought back a vague memory of playing in the mud with Nellie. When my mud toys dried, if they were small enough and I was careful, I could pick them up and take them back to the oak tree and my friends.

*   *   *

Cousin Stasia had a baby girl that summer. There were now six people in the family to feed and clothe. Money was scarce. A tobacco blight, a disease that caused the tobacco plants to wither and die, virtually eliminated my uncle's income. He had several mortgages on his farm, and he didn't receive any aid for keeping me. He was distracted and spoke very little, spending a great deal of time alone in the barn.

John Sullivan came over one afternoon, and he and JH talked quietly in the living room. Both of them were suffering financially. Uncle John left and came back two days later and met with JH again. I was certain they were talking about me and worried about what was going to happen.

*   *   *

On the morning of February 22, 1876, at the age of ten, I was told to stand by the window with Uncle JH and Cousin Stasia. No one spoke, but Cousin Stasia looked very grim and kept wiping tears from her eyes. A package containing all of my belongings was at my feet. I was excited yet fearful about what was in store for me. Obviously I was going somewhere. Maybe back to Uncle John's with Jimmy and Mary!

I soon heard a wagon approaching. Cousin Stasia gently led me out to the wagon, told me to get in, and handed me the parcel of my things. I climbed into the carriage, and to my surprise Jimmy was sitting there. Our driver introduced himself to us as Seth Bennett. Uncle JH said not a word to me and after a brief conversation with the driver reached into the carriage and squeezed my hand. He and Cousin Stasia stood quietly and watched us depart.

*   *   *

I was delighted to see Jimmy after what seemed an eternity since I had last seen him. We were both anxious because neither one of us had the faintest idea where we were going. But at least we were going together.

I asked him where Mary was, and he told me that Aunt Mary Cleary had come and taken Mary home with her. I squinted my eyes and tried to see everything I could on this mysterious adventure. I insisted that Jimmy describe everything he saw.

It was six miles from Feeding Hills to the Springfield train station. We arrived just as an enormous shiny black Western Railroad train whistle blew as it was puffing its way in to the station. Our driver lifted us down from the carriage, handed the horse and carriage over to another man, and led us into the station. I carried our parcels of clothing as Jimmy hobbled along painfully on his crutches.

After purchasing tickets, Mr. Bennett led us out on the platform and ushered us into one of the train cars. He motioned for us to sit on one of the wooden bench seats, and he sat in the seat just behind us. "All aboard" was shouted, and off we went.

We had never been on a train before, and our excitement replaced all of our fears. A wood-burning stove nestled in the corner of the car was smoky but made it nice and warm. It was ninety miles to Boston, and after the initial excitement of the ride, both of us were very weary. Mr. Bennett gave us each a slice of bread and some cheese. Jimmy cried in pain as the train car bumped and swayed. The smoke from the stove soon made my eyes sore and watery.

We both tried to get comfortable and attempted to sleep. I tried to hold Jimmy so his leg would be protected from hitting the hard wooden seat. He finally dozed off, but I was too uncomfortable to have the luxury of sleep. We must have been a sad sight. A young girl who was poorly dressed with swollen red eyes and a little crippled boy.

We arrived in Boston well after dark. It had been a very long day, and we were both exhausted. Two nuns approached us and after a brief conversation with Mr. Bennett took our parcels and led us to a horse-drawn carriage that would take us to the Tewksbury almshouse. That's the last time we saw Mr. Bennett.

7

ABOUT TEWKSBURY ALMSHOUSE

The Tewksbury almshouse (poorhouse) was located on 894 acres in Tewksbury, Massachusetts, about 105 miles from Feeding Hills, and about thirty miles from the coast. It was needed primarily because of the influx of Irish to the area following the famine. With the Depression in the United States, the Irish men could not find work. Towns all across the United States were stretched beyond their capacity to house and employ all of the immigrants.

The almshouse opened in May 1854 for the poor and was expected to house up to five hundred people. There were only fourteen employees. Within twenty days the population was over eight hundred, and by December of that year there were 2,193 people living there. It cost the state about $1.88 per person. Tewksbury was allotted $90,000 yearly to run the almshouse.

Captain Marsh was the head of the almshouse, and several of his family members worked there also. There were two other almshouses opened in Massachusetts at about the same time supported by the state. The immigrants were spread between the three almshouses. Ninety percent of the population of Tewksbury was Irish.

In 1866 they started accepting the insane. By 1874, two years before we arrived, 40 percent of the people there were considered insane, 27 percent required hospitalization, and 39 percent were there because they were poor and had nowhere else to go.

Social services under President Ulysses Grant had deteriorated during his second term; and there was corruption, scandal, and mismanagement throughout the administration. President Rutherford B. Hayes had his hands full trying to identify problems in the system and improve social services.

Tewksbury was seriously affected by the government's corruption. The superintendent submitted report after report that Tewksbury needed a great deal of help. Temporary buildings were needed; there was no barn to house cows that could supply much-needed milk to the wards and hold supplies in the winter. Everything needed paint, and the porches were insecure.

More separate wards were needed for the insane, those with contagious diseases, and patients subject to maniacal attacks. Water closets were needed in the wards to replace filthy chamber pots.

Rumors started spreading of atrocities at Tewksbury; and in 1879, three years after Jimmy and I arrived, Governor Butler ordered a full investigation into the conditions there.

Senator Gillmore led the investigation, and with him were six Republicans and three Democrats. Three were senators and eight representatives. Counsel for the almshouse was E. P. Brown, Esq.

Witnesses were called to testify over the several months of the investigation. One of the first findings was that of the $90,000 given to Tewksbury for maintenance of the almshouse, 70 percent or $63,000 was used for salaries which was about one-third more than should have been paid to salaries. Other atrocities shocked the entire country.

The bodies of patients that died and not claimed by family members were sold to medical students for $14. Babies and body parts were sold for $3. Coffins were dug up after burial and bodies removed for selling.

It was later discovered that even if family members claimed the body, many times a piece of wood was placed in the coffin instead of the body, and the body was sold. Profits went into the pockets of management of Tewksbury and the people delivering the bodies. One witness testified that he had purchased the skin from the back and one arm down to the fingertips of a human body. The skin had been tanned. It was found that this was also a common practice.

Rats, mice, and cockroaches infested the buildings crawling on the patients' beds as they slept. One witness reported that an insane woman's brain was eaten out by rats during the night.

Most of the food and milk purchased by Tewksbury went to the staff. Two hundred ninety-five pounds of butter were made per month in the dairy. Of this, only one pound per meal was allowed for the inmates. The rest went to the captain's kitchen or was sold by the staff for personal profit.

Patients had very little to eat, and the bread they were given was sour, and the quantities were small. Children cried themselves to sleep from hunger. Several of the bodies sold to medical students were found to have starved to death.

The investigation revealed that physicians were not called when patients were sick, but in actuality physicians and nurses were not paid adequately enough to make the trip to Tewksbury and attend to its many patients. The doctor did make occasional visits to tend to the people who needed care desperately and had a chance for survival.

It's interesting that at one time Tewksbury was lauded for its care and sometimes success with patients suffering from tuberculosis. Things obviously had deteriorated a great deal.

About seventy patients were bathed in the same water when many of them had running sores. The clothes of inmates were stolen and the material used to remake dresses for the matron's grandchildren.

Beds were made of straw and allowed to get filthy and rot. Some had only one sheet; some had nothing but a thin blanket. The insane women wore nothing but thin calico dresses. They had no underwear, shoes, or stockings. Sometimes they were left in their cells for days with only water. The cells appeared never to have been cleaned.

Morphine was given to the children at night to keep them quiet and make them sleep. In one year, seventy-two of the seventy-three babies housed at the almshouse died. Unwed mothers sent there to have their babies were given doses of some sort of medicine every fifteen minutes for twenty-four hours to encourage the birth. Many of the healthy young mothers died giving birth.

Prior to the investigation, visiting officials were always taken to one particular patient's room by the name of Honora O'Connor. Her room was clean, and she was well fed. She was used as the example for the entire facility.

In 1883, as a result of the investigation, a Mr. Fallen temporarily replaced Captain Marsh; and the arduous task of putting things in order at the almshouse began.

8

LIVING AT TEWKSBURY

From the Boston train station, we traveled the thirty miles to Tewksbury in a carriage called Black Maria, the hearse used to take bodies out of the almshouse. Jimmy and I huddled together on a wooden seat in the carriage. It was cold and very uncomfortable. The nuns were very quiet, probably concentrating on keeping warm and looking forward to their cots.

I was frightened and knew that I had to concentrate on protecting Jimmy and to make certain we would not be separated again. He was the only family I had left. He had been taken from me once, and I would not allow it again. After a very long journey, we arrived at our destination.

We drove through a vine-covered archway to the front of an enormous three-story building. It was eerily dark and gloomy. The nuns ushered us into the building through two large doors and left us in a dark hallway. I could not see clearly and didn't know where we were supposed to go.

I was startled when the shadow of a large man suddenly appeared before us. Jimmy was crying softly from both fear and the terrible pain of his leg. We were both cold and hungry. The man introduced himself as Captain Marsh and said he was the head of the almshouse. He took us into his warm, pleasant office.

There was a wonderful aroma of something he had just eaten in the room that made me realize how hungry I was. A steamy warm cup of liquid sat on the corner of his desk. We had only been fed bread and cheese since we had left Feeding Hills early that morning, and I was hoping for something good to eat. The room was so cozy that I allowed myself to relax a little, thinking this may be a fine place for Jimmy and me.

Jimmy was unable to sit because of the pain he was suffering, so we stood in front of Captain Marsh's desk while he asked us several questions. Where was our mom? Where was our dad? Did we have other family? What was wrong with my eyes? What was wrong with Jimmy's leg? He was finally satisfied with our responses and told us Jimmy would be going to the men's quarters and I the women's. Jimmy started wailing and clinging to me, and I cried and begged that we be allowed to stay together.

Since we were both unwell, we could not be placed with the other children that were there. Captain Marsh finally gave in and said we could stay together, but Jimmy would have to wear a smock if he were going to stay in the women's quarters. Jimmy didn't argue that he had outgrown smocks and wore breeches now because he was so afraid he'd be separated from me.

We were taken back out into the cold, dreary hallway and up two flights of stairs to the women's quarters on the third floor. By this time, Jimmy was in so much pain with his leg that he cried continuously. It took us a long time to climb the stairs. Thankfully Captain Marsh carried the packages of our clothing so I could use all my strength (which at this point was very little) to help Jimmy climb the stairs. I don't think Captain Marsh wanted to touch either of us.

When we got to the top of the stairs, two large doors greeted us for entry to our new home. What lay on the other side? Captain Marsh warned Jimmy to quit crying and be quiet because people were sleeping, and he didn't want them disturbed. He threatened that if we weren't quiet, Jimmy and I would be separated.

Jimmy pulled himself together, and with as much strength and courage as we could muster, we entered the women's ward. It had a foul odor of urine and unwashed clothing. It reminded me of our house on the Taylor farm when Mother was sick. Oh, how I yearned for my beloved mom.

I had experienced cleanliness at JH's home and didn't want to live in a filthy, stinky place again! It was cold and drafty, and on each side of the long room were rows of cots with sleeping figures on them. Tall windows lined the walls above the cots, letting in moonlight. Only a small kerosene lamp burned at the end of the room.

The only sounds were the snores and moans of the sleeping women and the unintelligible words of an obviously deranged woman who was shuffling around the room.

There were tables in the large aisle that ran down the center of the room between the rows of cots. We were ushered to a separate room in the back of the ward where there was a bed, a table with a pitcher of water, and some type of an altar with a cross. There was one sheet and a thin blanket on the bed. We were not offered any food.

We were shown a dirty chamber pot by the wall and ordered to quietly undress and go to bed. In the dark, we unpacked our meager belongings and put everything we owned on the table. We climbed into the bed and huddled together for warmth. I had to be very careful not to touch Jimmy's leg. I held Jimmy closely to comfort him until I felt his little body go limp and heard the soft sound of his relaxed breathing. Only then could I fall asleep myself.

*   *   *

The next morning I awoke to the rustling sounds of the women in the ward preparing for the day. I woke Jimmy up, and we cautiously left our little chamber. We entered the large room, and I got my first shadowy glimpse our house companions. All of the women were old and toothless; and many of them had dementia, yelled obscenities, and spoke nonsense. Some just aimlessly shuffled around the room.

The bedridden women had sores on their bodies and cried in pain. I learned quickly not to look closely at those wretched souls. From the odor, it was obvious that many of the women suffered from incontinence. I was reminded of the dirty diapers I had thrown out by the outhouse when Mother was too sick to clean.

A pleasant but harried matron came in and showed us two cots located in the middle of the ward that would be ours. Because there wasn't a water closet on our floor, we were directed to use the chamber pot at night. During the day, we could use the water closet located near the dining room or one of the outhouses behind the building. The chamber pot was to be emptied each day. We were to wash from one of the tubs of water located on the tables in the center of the room. There were also rows of zinc-lined sinks in small rooms on either end of the dining hall we could use when we went for meals. The bedridden used chamber pots that were emptied only occasionally. Usually not until they were full.

It was impossible for Jimmy to go up and down the stairs to the water closet, so he used the chamber pot, and I emptied it each day. We soon got used to the foul odors of the room.

We both jumped when there was a blast of a loud whistle. One of the women told us it was time to eat. The men went to the dining hall first. Suddenly the women who were able all raced to the windows to watch the men parade into the dining hall. I found out that this group of men was called the Horribles.

These men were all physically deformed in some way, some without limbs and others with terrible growths covering their bodies. Many suffered from insanity and yelled and fought like animals, racing and pushing to get to their food. Every mealtime the women raced to the windows to watch this bizarre parade.

The women pointed and laughed as the men prodded one another with canes and crutches and even clawed and bit one another. Several were given terrible names.

Finally one of the women told me it was our turn to go to the dining hall. We were starving since we hadn't eaten since midday the day before and were both eager to have some breakfast. I grabbed Jimmy's hand, and we followed the women toward the stairs for the journey to the dining hall. Those who were unable to get out of bed were left behind and would be brought food by one of the matrons. Unfortunately with the staffing problem at Tewksbury, sometimes this was much later in the day, and the food was always cold.

We went down the two flights of stairs and out a back door into a quadrangle of yard enclosed between the buildings. I later found out that when the weather was clear, people spent their days out on the grass soaking up the warm rays of the sun. I was excited to spend time out-of-doors again.

The dining hall was one of the buildings facing the quadrangle. As we entered, my mouth watered in anticipation of a meal. We followed a line along tables where food was dished out and handed to us. There were several large kettles on the tables with women standing behind them using ladles to spoon something into a bowl.

They gave each of us a small bowl and half a glass of watered-down milk. The bowl was about half full of cold, runny gruel. Somehow I managed to carry both our breakfasts, found a table for us, and helped Jimmy settle onto the bench. The gruel tasted as bad as it looked, but I was hungry and quickly had my breakfast eaten. Jimmy frowned but followed my example. It was enough to take the edge off our hunger.

Our meals gave our frail bodies a bit of nourishment and nothing more. Lunch was stale bread and broth and dinner stale bread and broth, and when we were lucky, the broth had an inkling of vegetables. Never meat.

Straining my eyes and looking around the dining hall, I noticed there were all ages of women sitting at our table. Since my sight was bad, Jimmy described everything he saw. There were young women with mental problems that would yell or talk to some ghost they saw in their heads. Some ate like animals, and several young unwed mothers quietly ate in shame awaiting the birth of their unwanted babies so they could leave Tewksbury.

The babies would be left behind and if they were lucky enough to survive may be adopted, but usually spent their lives at Tewksbury.

Several women sitting near me with hardly any hair had sores and growths all over their faces and arms. My stomach churned, and I quickly learned not to look at them and hurried to finish my meal and leave.

I must say though that there were also very nice women who gave us toothless grins and patted us on our heads. Others grumbled about having to eat with the children. Many of the men sneered at the women yelling obscenities and making filthy gestures, and some of the women yelled and gestured back.

That first morning, Jimmy used the stairs to eat in the dining hall, but it was just too difficult for him to make the journey down and up the stairs every day. He managed going down all right, but climbing back up the stairs was extremely painful for him. After our first day, the matron was kind enough to let me carry his food up to him so he wouldn't have to climb the stairs.

So what did we do the rest of the day? Jimmy couldn't go outside because he couldn't handle the stairs, so we started playing between our cots. There was hardly any space between the cots, and some of the women yelled at us to be quiet.

We looked at the room at the end of the ward where we had spent our first night. There was plenty of room for us to play on the floor there, so that room became our playroom. We found a stethoscope, a knife, tweezers, and some rolls of bandages we played with until the doctor visited one day and found us out. After that, he took his tools and supplies with him when he left.

I soon found out that this was the dead room where they took the bodies of people who died in the ward and kept them there until they were carried away for burial. We got used to having a silent covered companion on the table in the room with us waiting to be taken to their last resting place. Many of the women in the ward longed for that day for themselves. They wanted to be free from their lives of discomfort and pain. There was no grieving when one of them passed away.

As I climbed under my blanket on my cot after that first day, I pondered our situation. I was repulsed by many of the women; but at least most of them were Irish, I had a cot to sleep on, and most importantly, I had Jimmy. Tewksbury stank and was dirty, but we had lived in filthy conditions before.

I vowed that somehow we would manage living in this place and someday leave, live somewhere nice and clean, and go to school. I would not give up! I soon went to sleep with those determined thoughts on my mind.

*   *   *

Most of our days in Tewksbury were spent in our little room. The only time we couldn't play there was when the doctor came on one of his rare visits to tend to someone. Otherwise, interruptions to our play were our meals and my trips to the outhouse. We were left alone by the busy staff. They seemed grateful that we kept each other occupied and didn't cause them more work.

One of the matrons brought us scissors and old magazines to play with. We also had little friends in our playroom. There were pretty little dark brown mice and large black cockroaches that we were able to corner and catch.

The cockroaches would be forced to play games that I'm sure bewildered them and made to race against one another through a maze we made out of paper from the magazines. We had names for all of them. We tried making all kinds of traps to catch the little mice, but they usually outfoxed us. We never attempted to catch the rats though Jimmy did taunt and tease them. They would sit off in a corner and look at us through their beady little eyes daring us to approach them. Jimmy was braver than I when it came to the rats. We had heard how they crawled across people's beds while they were sleeping and bit them. I always checked my cot carefully before I crawled in just in case I had a rat bed partner waiting for me.

From the magazines, we cut out pictures of men, women, and children and made a family. Sometimes I found a picture of a school or school supplies, and we played school for hours from the memories I had from going to school with my friend Mary.

My eyesight was continuing to worsen, and there were times I had to have Jimmy cut out pictures from the magazines for me and explain the fine details. Some days were worse than others when my eyes were red and swollen and pained me to even try to open them.

Most of the women in the ward who were lucid were kind to us. When there was conversation between the women, they talked about the only thing they had in common, life in Ireland and the famine. I was eager to listen to their stories and learn about the land where Mother and Dad were born and raised. However, I soon got bored because they just kept repeating the same ones over and over again.

We became good friends with an elderly woman by the name of Maggie Carroll who read books to us. She had lived at Tewksbury since she was a young girl. She was so badly crippled with arthritis that she could hardly turn the pages of a book. Most times I did it for her. For some reason she was strapped to a board on her bed and had a rack someone had made her for her books so she didn't have to hold them. She was a very pleasant little woman and liked by everyone. When she was unstrapped from the board and made to sit up, she cried out in pain. I couldn't stand to see my friend cry and ran and hid in the playroom whenever they attended to her.

I never saw anyone visit her except the priest. Occasionally the matron would deliver books to her. When I had tantrums or yelled at one of the other women, she would gently call me over to her bedside and by just talking to me ease my mind away from my anger and pain.

She loved reading us books about the life of the saints, and after completing a story, we would discuss the story and its characters until we tired of it and started another. These were adult books, so when Maggie realized we didn't understand a passage, she would retell us in words we did understand. Jimmy was not as interested in the stories as I was and many times just played alone or insisted I play with him in the playroom.

Maggie made Tewksbury more bearable. When she tired of reading, she told me stories. We pretended she was a schoolteacher and I was going to her class. I think she loved our pretending as much as I did because it took her away from her surroundings and misery.

When I told her I was going to go to school someday, she warned me that like many people there, I might never leave Tewksbury, especially since I was blind. I angrily told her not to say that and assured her I was going to leave and go to school.

Once every couple of weeks, we looked forward to hot water being brought into the ward and placed in large tubs for us to bathe in. The matrons always had Jimmy and me go first because Jimmy needed their help. We were small enough we could sit and stretch out a bit in the tub. Jimmy was so frail and small he could almost completely immerse himself under water.

Many of the women could only dip cloths into the water to clean themselves or put one leg in at a time. I slowly lowered myself into the water and sighed with contentment as the warm water enveloped my body. I can't say we were ever real clean because we couldn't use soap since it would get the water dirty with soap scum. So in essence we just rinsed off.

My hair was a tangle of knots and rats and would have been impossible to comb. It hung in dirty, unruly strings down my back unless I was lucky enough to find something to use to tie it up and out of my way. My scalp itched from lice. Sometimes I snuck into the doctor's bag while he wasn't looking and took out a piece of bandage to use for a tieback. When I look back, I am certain he knew I had taken a bandage because his bag was never far from him, and I'm sure I didn't leave it as neat and tidy as he did.

*   *   *

We did have visitors one day. Dad and his younger brother, whom I had never met, stopped by to see us and gave us candy. Dad told us he was on his way to Chicago. After he told us he was not taking us with him, our conversation was awkward; he didn't know what else to say to us. I felt nothing but hatred and anger when I saw him. I said nothing but a surly thank-you when he gave me some candy. Jimmy clung to him and cried before he left. How could he leave us there!

9

JIMMY

Each day Jimmy's health seemed to deteriorate. The lump on his leg was getting larger, and he was getting weaker and weaker. The matrons quit trying to give him baths and just had me wipe his face, arms, and hands with a cool cloth when he was feverish.

They tried to get him to take sips of his soup or water, but most times he refused. I stayed close to his cot and whether he was awake or not told him stories I made up about Mother and Nellie and my good friends the faeries. I hadn't seen them for quite some time since the weather didn't allow me to wander outside. I was anxious to talk to my faerie friend Lily again and see if she could use any faerie magic to help Jimmy feel better.

Pretty soon Jimmy didn't respond when I talked to him, and he slept all the time. The doctor finally came and examined him. When he was finished with his examination, he called me into the playroom. Sitting on the table next to me, he told me that Jimmy would be going on a journey soon and that I would not have him here long.

I knew immediately what he was saying. I'd seen enough death in my ten years to know that it was taking Jimmy. I didn't say anything for a long time, and when the doctor got up to leave, I lunged at him screaming no! I screamed and screamed until the doctor grabbed my arms and threatened to take me out of the ward if I didn't stop.

The women in the ward were upset and frightened when they heard my screams, and many of them starting wailing and crying as well. During the next few days, I didn't leave Jimmy's side. It seemed unusually quiet in the ward—perhaps I just didn't hear any of the comings and goings, but I think the women were quieter and grieving with me and for me.

The matrons or one of the other patients brought me my meals so I wouldn't have to leave Jimmy's side. He never woke up or showed any signs that he even knew I was there. I just watched his frail little chest rise and fall slower and weaker as the days went by.

I slept the sleep of escape. So when they came in and took Jimmy's body to the dead room, our playroom, I didn't even hear them. When I awoke, the room was just beginning to see the light of day. His bed was gone. It was May 30, 1876. Jimmy had died in the night of tubercular meningitis. We had been at Tewksbury for three months.

How could I have slept through the passing of the only person I had left in the world that loved me and that I loved so dearly? I would never see the sparkle in his eyes or hear his contagious laugh again. I had no one to hug or touch. I was completely alone. I didn't want to get up. I wanted to go back to sleep and join the rest of my family in death.

I was quivering from shock when I managed to sit up on my cot. Everyone else was still asleep. I sat in the quiet of the early morning for a long time not knowing what I should do. Finally, I rose and went into our playroom and in the darkness could see the outline of my little brother's body lying on the table. I went over and gently put my hand on his cold cheek.

There was screaming, and the screaming didn't stop. Hands reached for me and dragged me out of the room where Jimmy and I had spent so many hours together. I collapsed on the floor and lay there a long time until one of the invalid women came and tried to get me up. She was too frail to help me much less to have gotten out of bed to come to me. I stood up, and clinging to each other for support, we made our way back to her cot where I sat in her arms, and she comforted me while I wept.

Dawn finally came, and when the matron came into the ward, she took me back to see Jimmy again. I got up on the table and lay beside him, holding his little body in my arms. After a few moments, the matron suggested we go outside and gather flowers for his coffin.

It was nearly June, and the wildflowers were in their finest form. She took my hand, and we walked out into the fresh air of a new spring morning. Nothing had stopped with Jimmy's death. The birds were all scurrying around gathering twigs to mend nests heavy with fledglings and gorging themselves with tasty worms and bugs to feed their young. Everything seemed surreal.

We walked far out into a meadow where wildflowers were brilliantly displaying their colors. I gently picked white daisylike bloodroot, purple geranium, white and purple hepatica, and even some yellow goatsbeard that stretches its little petals to the sun only in the morning. Green leaves were added to our bundle to complete the array of color.

We stopped just outside the ward buildings and picked some lilacs to add to our sweet bundle. We returned with our arms full of these beauties, and the matron held them while I carefully placed them around Jimmy's body.

I left the dead room with great reluctance and lay on my cot. I must have dozed off because I woke to the sounds of men bringing in Jimmy's coffin. Soon, they came out carrying that precious box. The doctor asked if I wanted to go to the graveyard with him. It didn't take long to get there. There was a path that led to an open area of dirt that was the cemetery.

There were no headstones, just little mounds of dirt where people were buried. We walked over to an open grave. There was no service, and Jimmy's little coffin was immediately lowered into the grave. The sound of the dirt hitting the box was almost too much for me to bear. I thought of my mother and Nellie, my precious sister. I had heard that sound too many times before.

Then it was over. The doctor was kind enough to stay there with me for a few minutes while I wept. One of the men who had carried Jimmy out brought some flowers for me to place on the grave.

From the corner of my eyes, I saw shadows, and I am certain it was Lily and my other faerie friends coming to help me grieve. It gave me comfort. I never went into our playroom, in the dead house, again.

10

SURGERIES

Shortly after Jimmy's death, the lady in the cot beside Maggie's died. The matron said I could change cots and sleep next to Maggie. I was delighted to be able to be closer to my good friend. Sometimes I would lie on my cot, and we would just talk.

The priest that normally visited Maggie did not come anymore and was replaced by Father Barbara. He was a nice-looking large man who showed a great deal of love and concern for all of the women in the ward. I always looked forward to his visits and followed him around like a puppy. He was like the father I didn't have.

Several weeks after we had become the best of friends, Father Barbara told me he was going to take me away from Tewksbury and have my eyes operated on in Lowell, Massachusetts, at the hospital of the Soeurs de la Charite. I couldn't bear the thought of leaving Maggie and was uncertain that any changes in my life could be an improvement over my life at Tewksbury. Could it be worse? I had been at Tewksbury one year.

Maggie encouraged me to get the operation with the suggestion that it may be successful and allow me to learn to read. Finally with the hope of seeing again and getting rid of the irritating bright colors that danced around in my eyes obscuring my vision, I agreed to the operation.

*   *   *

Early in the morning the following week, Father Barbara arrived at Tewksbury in his small carriage to escort me to the hospital in Lowell. I was very frightened. It was only about five miles from Tewksbury to Lowell, and soon I found myself entering a large hospital.

The cleanliness of the place took my breath. The walls were painted white, and the wooden floors were shining, they were so clean. I was taken into a room with two beds, a small table next to each, and a curtain that could be pulled closed to provide privacy for each patient.

The hospital sisters wore uniforms and beautiful spotless white bonnets. I was washed thoroughly and my wet, clean hair brushed and untangled. After putting on a hospital gown that was much too large for me, I climbed into the fresh, clean bed.

As I settled back against the soft pillow, I took a deep breath of the clean, fresh surroundings; and the fear I had felt before vanished. The sister left to continue her work with other patients. There was no one in the other bed in the room.

After a tasty lunch of thick, meaty soup, bread and butter, and a tall glass of fresh milk, the fatigue from my worry, excitement from the trip, and the activities of the morning caught up with me. Clean and with my full stomach and cozy bed, I soon dozed off.

I woke up with a start when I heard a man's voice saying, "Wake up, Anne, I need to look at your eyes." It was Dr. Savory. He completed the painful examination on my eyes and told me he would see me soon in the operating room. He was kind and assured me all would be well and before I knew it I would be back in my bed. My eyes were to be bandaged for a few days.

I was taken into surgery midafternoon and was soon back in my room. I was still heavily sedated and in my semiconsciousness heard terrible moaning and screaming accompanied with a putrid odor.

As I regained consciousness, I realized the screams and odor were not in my dreams but in the bed beside me. The closed curtains did not block the screams of pain from my roommate. She had been badly burned, and what I smelled was the smell of burned flesh.

With my eyes bandaged, it was totally dark, and I became very frightened. I had never heard or smelled anything so bad, even at Tewksbury! I tried to get out of bed and fell screaming to the floor. One of the sisters heard me and came running over to help me up. She held me close for a moment and whispered that they would move me to another room.

I was moved to a large room with several other beds occupied by older women. My bandages were askew, and my head had to be rewrapped. There was nothing I could do in my blindness but listen to the chatter of the women. Unfortunately all they talked about was the woman that was burned so badly and their memories of other burn stories. It was very depressing, and I was eager to have my bandages off and leave.

Two days later Dr. Savory came in to remove my bandages. The curtains were pulled closed so the light wouldn't be too bright. After the bandages were removed, he told me to open my eyes and tell him what I could see. I opened my eyes, and the colors that had been so bothersome before were gone, but my vision was so blurry that I was still nearly blind. The surgery had failed.

It is impossible to describe my disappointment. Would I live my entire life blind at Tewksbury almshouse? What else could I do, where else could I go?

Much later I heard that while I was in the hospital, Uncle John and Aunt Mary went to Tewksbury and were told that Jimmy was dead and I was gone. Were they going to take us with them? I will never know. But I hoped with all my heart that they had come for me and wanted me living with them. Maybe they would come back.

The days of healing passed pleasantly enough. The sisters were very good to me. They let me help fold their beautiful hats. I'm sure I folded them improperly, but they never complained. I was allowed to follow them as they made some of their rounds giving patients water and medicine.

Father Barbara came to see me regularly. He took me with him to the church next door, on long walks along the banks of the Merrimac, and to the hospital wards when he visited his patients. Next door in the grand St. Patrick's Church in his beautiful voice, he chanted the stories of the cross for me. One of my favorite outings was helping the sisters on their errands of mercy, carrying food baskets to the poor.

*   *   *

I recovered much too quickly, and it was time to leave the hospital. Father Barbara took me to the home of the Browns who lived in Boston. It was a dark, dismal large house. My only duty was to wash and dry the dishes. It was made quite clear to me that I was not to touch anything else.

Fortunately, I was only there a few long boring days before I was taken to the city infirmary for more operations on my eyes performed by Dr. Wadsworth and Dr. Williams.

*   *   *

The infirmary was a very nice hospital for the poor. It wasn't nearly as nice as Soeurs de la Charite, but it was clean, and the patients were treated with kindness. The majority of the patients were terminally ill. The head nurse was a wonderful woman by the name of Miss Rosa. Her pretty dark hair was tied in a bun on the back of her head. She was very petite and pretty and was always smiling and laughing with the patients and adored by all.

Miss Rosa taught me how to make lemonade. It was a privilege to be able to go to the icebox and chip off ice, squeeze the lemons, and add the sugar all by myself. I drank a lot of lemonade while I was there just for the fun of making it.

I had two more operations on my eyes. Neither of them worked. Father Barbara was transferred to another state, and the Browns didn't need me, so the only place I could go was back to Tewksbury. As Miss Rosa helped me get ready for my trip back to Tewksbury, I cried and clung to her, begging her not to send me back there. She tearfully held me in her arms and told me there was nothing she could do. I must return to Tewksbury.

11

BACK TO TEWKSBURY

The hearse from Tewksbury, the Black Maria, arrived to take me back to the almshouse. As I climbed aboard, the driver recognized me and asked me why I was going back to Tewksbury. When I told him, he just sadly shook his head. I never thought I would have to ride in this cold dark vehicle again! And here I was. I made an oath to myself that I would not live the rest of my life in Tewksbury. I would find a way out!

This time I was assigned to a ward with younger women. They were diseased, crippled, or insane. A few of them were covered with syphilis sores. It was nice to be with young girls my age and have playmates.

Our ward matron's name was Maggie Hogan. She was a kind, sweet little old woman with a very crooked back. She seemed very fond of all her young charges. Everyone called her Little Mother.

Across the hall from my ward, there was a large ward full of women who were pregnant. Most of them were prostitutes. Their stories and language fascinated me. They took turns reading stories of rape, murder, and other crimes from the *Police Gazette*, and I hung on every word.

I was introduced to subjects and words no eleven-year-old should know. At this stage of my young life, nothing shocked me. Maggie Hogan tried in vain to keep me away from those wretched women. However, I continued to go to their ward and listen to their chatter. I was just too curious, and there wasn't anything else to do.

I heard all about sexual acts, jokes about their sex partners, and all the places where the acts were performed, from closets to alleys. They also read the *Boston Pilot*, whose editor was Irish, to learn how the Irish were faring in America. This especially interested me.

There were several young women who had been seduced or raped and were quietly waiting for their babies to be born. After their babies were born, they were sent to the workhouse in Bridgewater. If they were lucky, they found jobs in private homes. Unfortunately many of them returned to Tewksbury to have more babies.

Beefy, the supervisor of the dining room, was always making crude remarks, fondling and touching the women and girls when we went to eat. Some of them returned the caresses and joked with him. For those who didn't, complaining did no good. I had to sidestep him many times to keep his hands from me. It was rumored that some of the women got pregnant at Tewksbury. I wouldn't be surprised. There were many occasions when I had to fight off men to stop them from touching me.

Several times, when I went outside for my walks and fresh air, I ran into an insane boy whose name was Jimmy Burns. He seemed safe enough because the matrons trusted him to run errands for them. He and I gradually started talking and became friendly. I loved his deep masculine voice.

One day he approached another girl and me as we were walking together and started flirting with us. It started off innocently enough, but my friend was afraid of him and ran off. I stayed, and he reached up and touched my cheek, begging me to fly away with him. I jokingly said I'd meet him tomorrow and we'd fly off to a magic place somewhere. Then it turned more serious, and the look on his face changed, and he demanded that I kiss his "Jennie."

He grabbed me and pulled me close to him and kissed me. He finally let me go, and I hurried back to my ward. I told everyone what had happened. Maggie Hogan warned me to stay away from him because he could indeed be dangerous.

A few days later, I saw Jimmy on the grounds again and thought it was foolish to be afraid of him. He seemed harmless. When he saw me, he came running toward me, yelling my name in a strange voice with that odd look on his face again. As I turned to say I needed to get back to my ward, Jimmy grabbed me roughly and pulled a large bread knife out from under his coat.

My screams attracted the attention of another man who wrestled Jimmy to the ground and told me to run. I wasted no time getting back to the ward. I kept a wary eye out for Jimmy every time I stepped out of the ward after that. It made my outings a little less enjoyable because I had to stay where there were always other people present and couldn't go off by myself.

I still visited with my friend from my old ward, Maggie Carroll. She loved to have me come and listen to her read and tell her what was going on outside of her ward.

Maggie Hogan, my ward matron, introduced me to a little library on the first floor of our building; and we found books written by Irish men and women. She encouraged one of the girls in our ward named Tillie to read to me. She was the only girl there who knew how to read, though she didn't like to and had to be bribed. Tillie always talked about escaping from Tewksbury, so in order to get her to read, I told her I would help her escape.

After reading, she would demand I share my escape plans with her. I had to go so far as to sneak out with her at night and pretend to look for an escape route. When none were found, we would return to our beds with a promise from me that I would come up with another plan.

Maggie actually helped me with the escape plans. Several times Maggie told Tim, the guard, to leave the gate open and when Tillie ran out, catch her and return her. She always thought we had planned a great escape.

Tillie read in a monotone, and I had to listen carefully because sometimes she skipped paragraphs or entire pages. Every once in a while she got very quiet and began to shake all over, foam at the mouth, and make strange noises. The first time this happened, I ran and got Maggie. She told me that Tillie had these fits occasionally and not to worry about her. They would just pass. I learned to sit quietly and wait for the fit to cease, and then she would continue reading. Sometimes she was tired after one of her fits and had to go lie down.

When I went to the library, the superintendent read the titles to me, and I picked out my own books. Some of books I picked were *Cast Up by the Sea, Ten Nights in a Barroom, The Octoroon, The Lamplighter, Darkness and Daylight,* and *Tempest and Sunshine.* Maggie Carroll sometimes read them to me, but she preferred reading the stories of the saints.

Another girl joined our ward named Delia. After her mother died in Ireland, she ran away from home and, after living with several men, was brought by one of them to America. He died soon after they arrived, and she ended up in Tewksbury. Delia knew how to read and took turns with Tillie reading to me.

No more operations on my eyes were offered. Doctors visiting Tewksbury never even looked at my eyes. Everyone gave up, and I was destined to be blind. However, deep down inside I knew I absolutely wouldn't remain at Tewksbury for my entire life.

I quit saying anything to the others because they would just scoff and tell me I needed to just accept the fact that I would spend my life there.

I wouldn't believe it and still lived with the hope to learn to read and go to school.

I had been at Tewksbury for over four years. I was fourteen and getting desperate.

*   *   *

It was a beautiful, crispy fall day; and after a wonderful walk in the fall air, I went to visit my old friend Maggie Carroll. She told me that there was going to be an investigation of Tewksbury because word had gotten out that there were horrible things happening here. A Mr. Frank Sanborn was supposedly coming the next day. He was the chairman of the State Board of Charities.

She suggested I approach him and tell him I'd like to go to school. I thought she was daft and reminded her that I was blind. She told me there was a school for blind children in Boston called Perkins School for the Blind. My heart soared! Could this possibly be my chance to get out of this place?

I don't think I heard a word Maggie read that day. I could think of nothing but how I would approach Mr. Sanborn.

I slept very little that night thinking of every possible scenario for approaching Mr. Sanborn. Morning finally arrived, and I washed up and positioned myself on the first floor just inside the doors so I could see Mr. Sanborn arrive. I didn't eat breakfast or lunch. After an eternity, I saw a blurry group of important-looking men in fancy suits came through the door right in front of me.

I lost all courage. They were very grave and somber. After they had talked to the superintendent in his office, they walked right past me again and began their tour of Tewksbury. No one noticed me sitting there.

I followed them all over the premises that day. When I couldn't follow them into buildings that were off limits to me, I hid just outside the door and waited for them to come out.

After they inspected the last building, they returned to the main building and prepared to leave. I knew that I must approach Mr. Sanborn right then. I didn't know for certain which man was Mr. Sanborn. The man that everyone seemed to follow donned his hat and walked out the door. He was nearly to the gate when I conjured up all the courage I had and went running out to him and cried, "Mr. Sanborn, I want to go to school!"

He was very cold and serious when he asked me what was wrong with me and how long I had been at Tewksbury. I nervously told him my name was Anne Sullivan, I was nearly blind and had been there for over four years. Mr. Sanborn turned to leave, and I grabbed his coat, begging him to let me go to school. He released himself from my grasp and left.

My heart sank. He didn't take me with him! I slowly walked back to the ward and lay on my cot until supper. After supper I went to see Maggie and told her what had happened. She told me not to give up. He may just send for me. I went to bed very despondent, knowing that if this didn't work, I'd be at Tewksbury for the rest of my life.

I spent most of the next day sitting amongst the roots of my favorite tree, seeking solace. A woman from the administration office approached me and told me I was to hurry and pack because I was leaving Tewksbury and going to school. I was shocked and for a moment just sat there. Then the reality of it all sank in, and I jumped up and followed her into the ward to prepare to leave.

I had no clothes, so the matron went through the wards and gathered up everything she could find that might fit me. I ended up with two new dresses, one red and one blue with flowers on it; two pairs of worn black stockings; and a pair of scuffed shoes that were a little to small for me.

There was one more stop to make before I left. I ran upstairs to say goodbye to my dear friend Maggie Carroll. I gingerly reached down and hugged her, and our tearstained faces touched for the last time. She shooed me away and told me to be good and mind my teachers.

*   *   *

Carrying my little bundle of clothes, once again I climbed into the Black Maria. I turned, and a crowd of my Tewksbury friends were waving to me and wishing me well. Before I got into the carriage, the driver, Tim, turned and said to me, "Don't ever come back to this place. Do you hear? Forget this and you will be all right." But nothing would ever erase the terror and filth scored upon my mind during my years at Tewksbury. I was fourteen years old.

What had I learned at Tewksbury? I learned about hatred and cruelty. I learned distrust. I learned about hunger, deformities, perverts, filth, and death. Exposure to the horrible conditions that occurred in my first fourteen years on this earth affected me my entire life. I struggled to put the images of my childhood behind a wall in my mind, hoping to never let them see daylight. But the resulting anger, resentment, and feelings of inadequacy always plagued me. My experiences would never be forgotten, and those memories forced their way into my thoughts many times over my lifetime.

12

HISTORY OF PERKINS SCHOOL FOR THE BLIND

In the early 1800s, blind people were thought to be unable to live normal lives and work so therefore should not be educated. They were usually dependent totally on their families or institutionalized.

Dr. John Dix Fisher, a pleasant, energetic young man with curly hair, studied medicine in Paris in the 1820s. He was especially interested in the blind. While in Europe, he visited the National Institution for Blind Youth. He was impressed when he discovered that they taught the blind all of the subjects taught in regular schools. At the time, there were only two schools in the United States for the blind, one in New York and the other in Philadelphia. These schools were founded on the premise that blindness was an act of God, and those who were blind were unable to learn. The schools were more like institutions.

After he visited the schools in Europe, Dr. Fisher disagreed with the American philosophy regarding the blind. He was determined to establish a school in the Boston area where children could be taught to read and write and care for themselves. Dr. Fisher, along with several of his influential friends, convinced the Massachusetts legislature that a blind school was necessary. An act incorporating the New England Asylum for the Blind was signed on March 2, 1829.

After two years of searching for a director for the school, Dr. Fisher was very pleased when a college friend, Dr. Samuel Gridley Howe, accepted the offer to direct the school. Dr. Howe was a handsome, popular young man known for riding around Boston on his beautiful black stallion. He married Julia Ward Howe in 1843. She was the author of the "Battle Hymn of the Republic," a poet, and very active in the community and later at the school.

Mr. and Mrs. Howe were determined to make positive changes in the world. As a young man, he joined the freedom fighters in Greece. He was later known for his work to improve the education and quality of life for the blind, the deaf, and the feebleminded. He fought for prison reform and antislavery and held positions on boards of the Sanitary Commission, the Massachusetts Board of State Charities, and Massachusetts General Hospital. He was energetic, a born leader, and anxious to devote his time to yet another endeavor—the New England Asylum for the Blind.

The first thing Dr. Howe did was sail to Paris to study the techniques used in the schools for the blind in Europe. He returned with two teachers who were blind. Emile Trencheri was hired for academics and John Pringle for mechanical trades. Both were excited to be taking key roles in the establishment of the new school.

Dr. Howe's family lived in a large home in Boston. Several rooms of their home were used as classrooms for the first seven blind students who attended the school.

With no money and only three raised-print books, Dr. Howe was forced to make his own teaching material. Most of the children arrived at the school in poor health, primarily because they were treated like invalids and did not get enough exercise or fresh air.

Dr. Howe insisted on a vigorous exercise program for all of the children as well as academics. The children thrived under his care. To be able to continue the school, however, it was critical to obtain more funds. Dr. Howe realized that the only way he could raise funds was to have more publicity.

The children were paraded before the Massachusetts legislature. Legislators were very impressed when the healthy, happy children entered the room with confidence and showed off their math and reading skills and knowledge of geography. They immediately agreed to allocate money for the school. Word got out about the New England Asylum for the Blind, and soon the Howe home was much too small. Now that there were funds, Dr. Howe started looking for new quarters for his school.

Thomas Perkins heard about the school and its need for larger quarters and approached Dr. Howe with an offer to loan his mansion on Pearl Street in Boston if the school could raise and match funds. This was accomplished with private donations and public support.

In six years, the school had sixty students and many on a waiting list. The mansion was sold and the proceeds used to purchase an old five-story wood-frame hotel in south Boston.

In 1839 the new school opened with the new name of Perkins Institute for the Blind to honor the generosity of Mr. Perkins. Dr. Howe was delighted with the new quarters. There were miles of walking trails, and it was close enough to the ocean for the children to swim—something previously unheard of.

One of Dr. Howe's most famous accomplishments was breaking through the darkness of a deafblind young girl by the name of Laura Bridgman. She and I were to become good friends.

Dr. Howe was also chairman of the State Board of Charities in Massachusetts, and his last official act in that position was in favor of an investigation of the Tewksbury almshouse where I was living. Mr. F. B. Sanborn, the man I begged to let me go to school, was his good friend and successor to the State Board of Charities.

A young man by the name of Michael Aganostopoulos married Dr. Howe's eldest daughter and replaced Dr. Howe as director of Perkins School for the Blind when Dr. Howe died in 1876, four years before my arrival at the school. He went by the name Michael Aganos when he moved to America from Turkey.

13

LIFE AT PERKINS

On October 7, 1880, a state charity official accompanied me by train on my trip to Boston. I was fourteen years old. He never told me his name. At one of the train stops, a woman walking by us paused and asked me where I was from and where I was going. Before I could respond, to my horror, my escort told her I was from the Tewksbury almshouse. I know my face turned scarlet red in shame. To make matters worse, the woman patted me on my head and said "poor child" and gave me an apple with some bread and butter.

I realized at that moment that I must have looked very poor and ugly. The dress I had on was too big, my black stockings had holes in them, and my shoes were worn. When I left Tewksbury, I felt very beautiful, but not now. My excitement suddenly turned to shame and fear. I felt very insecure and terrified at what lay ahead.

We arrived in Boston in the late afternoon. The days were short, and it was just beginning to get dark. I was very tired from the excitement of the journey and the apprehension I felt with this major change in my life. My eyes were painfully red and sore, and my vision was extremely blurry.

I had never been to a large city before, and the sounds and shadows surrounding the carriage overwhelmed me. When we finally arrived at Perkins Institute for the Blind, I could see the outline of a very large building that would now be my new home. I found out later that it was a five-story wood-frame structure that had once been a hotel.

I was reminded of my arrival at Tewksbury, going through the large gates up to the doors of a tall dark building. Hopefully, this would be much different than Tewksbury. What awaited me here?

* * *

I took a deep breath of the crisp fall air just before I was ushered through large double doors down a hallway into a small room. I saw the outline of a man as he stood from behind a large wooden desk and greeted me warmly. He walked around the desk and stood close to me so I could see him. He told me his name was Mr. Aganos, director of the school. I could see that he was a tall man with short hair and a beard that went down to his chest. The soft lights from the lamps and the warmth of the room relaxed me somewhat. Mr. Aganos encouraged me to explore his office, which was on the first floor in a corner of the building. There were large windows on two sides of the room. Potted plants sat on the sills of the windows. I imagined it was quite light and cheerful during the daytime.

Mr. Aganos asked me several questions about myself. With a great deal of shame and trepidation, I told him that I was from Tewksbury almshouse, I didn't know how to read or write, I didn't know my numbers, and I had never been to school. I didn't even know my date of birth.

I couldn't stop myself and tearfully told him about the woman on the train and that I only had one other dress that was too big for me, and my shoes hurt my feet terribly. Fortunately he did not act shocked and spoke to me very kindly. He told me that they would find me some clothes and shoes that fit and assured me that I would be happy here and make good friends.

He took me on a tour of the school and explained to me what was in the various rooms. The students and teachers all lived in little cottages around the school yard with a housemother in each. The bedrooms were pleasant and clean. There were two beds on either side of a pretty window, a dresser, a desk, and a clothes closet. He explained that the girls did all the housework as part of their training and sewed their own bed linens. A hired staff prepared the meals and served them in the dining room where students sat at small round tables. The classrooms were large airy rooms with tall windows that were open whenever possible to let in fresh air. There were large tables in the middle of the room surrounded by chairs for the students. One of the rooms had a large puzzle that Mr. Aganos said was a picture of the United States. Another room had books with raised dots for letters, which allowed the blind children to read. I was elated! I would finally learn to read, even though I was nearly blind!

There was a gymnasium, and Mr. Aganos explained that the children all wore gym clothes and climbed ropes and ladders, played games, and ran races. On nice days, exercises were outside in the courtyard.

I was taken to my first class where a teacher was giving the girls singing lessons. All of the children in my class were six and seven years of age. I had to start with the lower grade level since I had never been to school. The teacher asked my name and then, to my horror, asked me to spell it. When I told her I couldn't spell, the children began laughing. I was asked my age, and when I told her I was fourteen, there was more laughter. A fourteen-year-old could not even spell her own name! Even the teacher laughed. I was embarrassed, disappointed, and miserable and felt that coming to this school had perhaps been a big mistake.

That was my first impression of Perkins. That night after supper, I was glad to get into my assigned bed. My roommate put on a nightgown and crawled into bed. I stood there shamefully, not knowing what to do because I didn't have a nightgown. This kind girl realized I was just standing there and asked me what was wrong. When I told her I didn't have a nightgown, she gave me one of her beautiful clean gowns to sleep in. I had never worn a nightgown before. I mumbled an embarrassed thank-you and climbed into my bed between clean white sheets under a warm quilt and let my tears silently flow.

I wasn't sure I could bear this. I was different from all of the other girls. None of them came from a poorhouse. They had nice clothes. I was in a classroom with six-and seven-year-old children, and I was fourteen. They all knew how to read, and I couldn't. What shame and embarrassment I felt. I was homesick for my friends at Tewksbury. How I wished I could talk to my friend Maggie Carroll.

I felt so terribly alone and out of place that night.

*   *   *

At five-thirty the following morning, when our housemother woke me, I approached the day with new resolve. I told myself I must persevere and learn to read and write! If these children at age six could, I certainly could. I was just as capable as anyone there, even if I did come from the poorhouse! I must succeed. I couldn't and wouldn't spend my life at Tewksbury!

To my delight, the housemother brought me a dress, underwear, stockings, and shoes to wear. Everything smelled nice and clean, and I felt more comfortable knowing my clothes fit me and I was like the other girls.

The clothes and shoes were used, but to me they were new. The two dresses I brought from Tewksbury I stuffed in the very back of the closet.

I joined the other children of our cottage in the dining room, and we had a wonderful breakfast of sweet warm porridge and cream. During breakfast, I heard a lot of whispers and giggles and knew they were directed at me, but I resolved not to care.

At six-thirty, breakfast was over, we washed our dirty dishes and tidied our bedrooms and made our beds. Then the children my age went off to their classrooms laughing and talking amongst themselves, and I silently followed the first graders to class.

Our days were very busy. We attended classes from 6:30 a.m. to 6:00 p.m. followed immediately by a delicious supper. It had been over four years since I had regular decent meals. At the school, we had oatmeal and cream for breakfast; soup and sandwiches for lunch; and meat, potatoes, and vegetables for dinner. Whatever fruits and vegetables were in season were on our menu. We were encouraged to drink a large glass of fresh, cool creamy milk at each meal. It didn't require coaxing for me to drink my milk. Whole milk that wasn't watered down was a real treat for me. There was an abundance of fresh baked bread; and sometimes we even had rich desserts of cake, fruit pie, or cookies.

I enjoyed exercise period especially when the weather was nice and we were able to go outside. I missed my long days out-of-doors. We learned to jump rope and gulped the clean, fresh air as we ran races in the courtyard that was surrounded by pear trees, apple trees, and beautiful pines. How wonderful it smelled in the spring when the fruit trees blossomed. When weather permitted, we even swam in the ocean. I actually found myself joining in and playing with the other children. We certainly weren't treated as invalids at Perkins. We were encouraged to do everything sighted children could do. We thrived with good health.

When it was cold and we couldn't go to the ocean, we quickly jumped into large vats of cold water in the basement. This tradition had been followed since the school opened because the founder, Dr. Howe, thought it was necessary for good health. We hated the cold water, but we certainly were always clean and healthy.

We exercised in the gym that was located in the basement of the building wearing baggy bloomers, middy tops, and tights. There were ropes to climb, obstacle courses to find our way through, ball playing, and race running. All of these exercises were meant to enhance the use of all of our senses, give us the ability to find our way around, play, and encourage us to do things on our own.

There was music instruction for voice, as well as piano, guitar, organ, and drums. I chose to learn to play the piano.

Evenings and weekends were spent in the large living room of our cottage where the girls read, sang, sewed, played games, talked, and wrote letters home. There were dolls for each girl, and I was thrilled at the age of fourteen to have my first doll. Because of my sour disposition and quick temper and anger, I was not well liked and usually spent my free time off in a corner with my doll and later when I could, read. I very rarely joined group activities except in gym.

Sunday, of course, was church day; and we were paraded to the various churches in the area depending upon our faith. I had no knowledge or interest in religion. I was required to attend church and accompanied the girls to the nearby Gate of Heaven Catholic Church for Sunday school. I found it boring and too structured. It was something I was forced to do, which made me surly and uncooperative. The Sunday school teachers soon learned to just ignore me and didn't include me in their discussions.

We had several different schoolteachers who taught our various subjects. Raised-dot reading, writing, math, and geography were all taught, as well as sewing (including how to thread a needle), personal hygiene, and basics of getting around on our own.

Unfortunately I was unable to keep up in any of the first-grade classes. Not even mat weaving! I had to live with the fact that I was way behind in my learning, which only made me angrier and more difficult.

I ignored as much as possible the taunting of the other children and worked very hard to catch up with them. However, I couldn't control myself and lost patience regularly and responded angrily to the teacher or another student. Sometimes I threw things and stomped my feet. When this happened, I was scolded and privileges taken away. That usually put me in a sulk, and I wouldn't talk to anyone or respond to any of the teacher's questions.

On one occasion after one of my outbursts, I remember a teacher making me stand in a closet with a skeleton used to teach the children about the human body. If she thought it would scare me, she didn't have the slightest idea of what I had seen at Tewksbury! I didn't like the teachers, and most of them didn't like me. I was a loner and became very melancholy. Several times a day teachers would have to reprimand me.

One day during math, I couldn't compute an equation Miss Moore asked me to solve, and the other children started laughing at me. I yelled at them to shut up and leave me alone. Miss Moore ordered me to leave the room and sit on the stairs and wait for her. I angrily got up from my desk, pushed another desk and chair out of my way, and headed for the door.

I was told to return to my desk and then leave the room the proper way, but I just turned and yelled, "I won't, I won't sit on the stairs, and I'll never return to this class again!" Of course, I slammed the door when I left. I ran to my cottage and threw myself on my bed.

A while later Mr. Aganos sent an older girl to escort me to his office. I was still angry and stomped down to his office with my head held high and made sure I had defiance written all over my face. He gave me the option to either behave myself and go back to my class or be expelled and return to Tewksbury. It was late in the afternoon, and Mr. Aganos told me I had the night to think about it. My defiance evaporated.

I left Mr. Aganos's office feeling defeated. I knew that this school was my only chance to have a life outside of Tewksbury. It was my only chance to learn to read and write. At supper I didn't even hear the other children. I was too caught up in my own thoughts. I knew I must be brave and courageous and work hard to achieve what I wanted so badly—to be able to read and write. I must.

The next morning I returned to my classroom. After classes were over, Miss Moore asked me to stay to chat. She told me that she understood how difficult it must be to be fourteen and in a classroom with six-and seven-year-olds. But I didn't really have a choice. I had to start learning from the beginning.

She told me that she had talked to Mr. Aganos, and they agreed that she could work privately with me an hour a day to help me learn more quickly and catch up with the other children my age. I was told I would have to hold my temper and be pleasant for this to work. I promised her I would do whatever she asked if she would teach me to read and write. I was moved by her kindness. She actually seemed to care about me.

I attended the regular classroom each day and after classes spent an hour with Miss Moore. First, we concentrated on reading. With a great deal of determination, I began working with Boston Line Type where each letter of the alphabet is created in miniature using raised dots on paper. The concept of the alphabet came easily to me. Reading the raised-dot books was more difficult because at an older age, the tips of my fingers weren't as sensitive as they would have been at the age of six. I had to work a little harder to feel the patterns on the paper, but in time and after many hours of practice, I was able to read. I was thrilled when I learned my first few letters and words. I was given a wooden board with grooves embedded in straight lines at regular intervals across it and learned when a piece of paper was laid on the board the grooves became lines to write on. My left index finger guided my pencil, and I was soon able to write square-hand printed letters.

Before long, I knew my numbers and had mastered addition and subtraction. Understanding their concepts took a little longer, but with Miss Moore's help and patience, within a few months I understood multiplication and division as well. I became more confident and actually began making a few friends.

I did my best to control my anger and attitude, but I must say that Miss Moore had more patience than you can imagine. I was determined to do everything perfectly and did not take criticism well. Errors in grammar or sentence structure would cause me to lose my temper. I got very angry with myself when I made mistakes.

On those numerous occasions, I was sent away to be alone until I could be civil. When I returned, Miss Moore always pleasantly welcomed me back and reminded me how remarkable it was that I was learning everything so quickly. I loved our times together. I was always anxious to see her at the end of our class days to share what I had learned. If my day had not gone well, or a teacher had reprimanded me, we discussed what other choices I could have made to avoid the confrontation. I listened to Miss Moore and followed her suggestions. As a result, I began to have fewer problems with the teachers and other students.

Our first summer vacation came much too quickly, and I had nowhere to go. One of my friends invited me to go to her home for the summer. She lived on a large farm in New Hampshire. I did not care for her odd parents and avoided them as much as possible. Even so, I enjoyed following my friend around the farm and visiting all of the animals. We shelled fresh peas and shucked corn while sitting in the swing on the front porch and helped in the kitchen and with chores as much as possible. Being in the out-of-doors and feeling the warmth of the sun, inhaling the wonderful aroma of the flowers, and hearing the rustle of the breeze through the massive trees with my friend made for a pleasant summer.

14

LAURA BRIDGMAN

In the fall, upon my return to Perkins, I was assigned a room with a blind/deaf woman by the name of Laura Bridgman. She was fifty-two years old and had lived at Perkins since 1836 when she was eight. The first director of Perkins, Dr. Howe, had gained fame for developing a method to teach her to communicate.

Laura had scarlet fever as an infant, leaving her with only the sense of touch. She did not even have the senses of smell or taste. Soon after she arrived at Perkins, Dr. Howe began her education by giving her objects she was familiar with and attached a raised-dot label to each, showing the name of the object. In just a couple of months, she was able to associate the label with the item. He then made labels with individual alphabet letters on them and piled them in front of her, and when handed an object, she found the letters to spell the name of the object.

With this new comprehension of language, she learned the names of everything around her. He then taught her to "talk" by teaching her how to spell words through using her hands. With her fingers, she spelled each letter of a word she was communicating into the listener's hand. The listener then answered by spelling back into Laura's hand. With this accomplished, Laura started attending classes with the help of an interpreter.

Laura's family could not take care of her, and she could only survive with an interpreter at her side. She was a permanent resident of Perkins.

She helped with housework and was accomplished at needlework. Her needlework was sold to provide her with income to purchase clothing and other personal iteMiss She loved to read and over the years had made many friends at the school with whom she kept in touch through letters written in square-hand print.

Laura and I became friends. I quickly learned how to fingerspell to her, and we were able to carry on conversations.

15

SCHOOL AND MORE SURGERIES

The second school year went by quickly. I enjoyed every subject except mat weaving and sewing, which I failed miserably! I loved to study and eagerly absorbed everything I was taught. I became a star pupil. Not that I didn't have my problems. Bouts of depression, impatience, and anger still tormented me. I was nearly expelled on several occasions during my time at Perkins. A few kind teachers and my housemother, Mrs. Hopkins, somehow managed to intercede and keep me there.

It was soon summer vacation again, and Mr. Aganos arranged for me to stay at a boardinghouse in Boston in exchange for light housework. It was a pretty large home with porches all around it where the boarders sat and enjoyed the summer evenings. Everyone was kind to me, and I enjoyed my stay there.

While there I made friends with a nice, intelligent young man, and we talked about all of the books and poetry we had read. He had acquaintances in the medical profession and made arrangements for me to go to the free clinic to have my eyes checked. I wasn't interested in pursuing another surgery after the previous ones had failed to restore my vision. It took him quite a while to persuade me to go.

I soon found myself perched on a table at the clinic with a doctor examining my eyes. I was doing this for my friend at the boardinghouse and had no hope of having any success getting my vision restored. After a lengthy, painful examination, the doctor announced that there was a good chance specialists at the Massachusetts Eye and Ear Infirmary could improve my vision.

The following week my friend accompanied me to the eye and ear infirmary for examination by Dr. Henry Withington Bradford. After his examination, he told me that several thousand cases like mine had been successfully treated.

On August 6, 1881, at the age of fifteen, I was admitted to the Carney Catholic Hospital for surgery on my left eye. I didn't let myself get excited about the prospect of regaining my sight because I had been so disappointed before. The surgery was performed followed by a long, slow recovery process. Gradually during the three months I was confined to the hospital, the eyesight in my left eye improved.

I spent a great deal of time at the window looking at the Charles River. Every week the sight in my left eye became clearer. By the time I left on November 1, 1881, I was able to make out letters on the printed page. I could use my vision to read! I cannot describe the intense joy I felt. I excitedly studied every object and face around me. I could hardly wait to see the wonder of the trees and flowers again. I had lived in pain and semidarkness for nine of my fifteen years.

*   *   *

I returned to classes at Perkins with joy and enthusiasm. I immediately began reading the raised letters instead of feeling them with my fingers. I read everything I could get my hands on that had large-enough print. I continued to excel in my studies and finally reached my grade level. For the first time in my memory, I was happy and enjoying my life.

I still suffered from bouts of anger and depression that I couldn't seem to control. Fortunately my teachers, Mr. Aganos, and my housemother, Mrs. Hopkins, stayed by my side and helped me through my difficult times.

Mrs. Hopkins became like a mother to me. She was a widow who had recently lost her daughter and went to work at Perkins to keep busy. She and I became very close. I spent my remaining four summers with her at her home in Cape Cod. What a glorious place! We explored, fed the seagulls, and sat on the beach, warm evenings watching the waves roll in, illuminated by the moon. She told me stories about her father and her late husband's voyages as sea captains and showed me treasures from all over the world. The summers flew by!

*   *   *

A year later, on August 7, 1882, Dr. Bradford operated on my right eye. This operation was also successful, and I regained the use of my right eye. I could now read 12-point print!

Fortunately, I was allowed to continue my studies at Perkins even though I was sighted. When I returned to Perkins, I began to read books only visually. Most of my free time was spent at the library. I excelled in all of my classes. My favorite course was Shakespeare. I loved the wonderful symphony of romance and words in the various parts of his plays. I especially loved his poetry though and tried my own hand at writing.

With my new sight, I was able to run errands, take walks, and again enjoy the array of color in the beautiful out-of-doors. I watched everyone busily traveling to and fro and stared in amazement at the numerous buildings of the city. I helped the teachers oversee some of the children's activities and took them to church. I never enjoyed church and didn't spare my opinions with the priest. It came to the point where Mr. Aganos asked me to please sit quietly with the girls at church and not share my opinions. I reluctantly agreed.

During my six years at Perkins, Mr. Aganos and I had many ups and downs in our relationship. But I admired him and could talk to him. I considered us friends. I did not like his wife or his mother-in-law, Julia Ward Howe. Both of them were always at the school.

His mother-in-law came to the school on an occasional Saturday and insisted that the girls all attend her reading of the *Iliad* or some other difficult work. The girls hated giving up their free time on Saturday to listen to her stuffy renditions. I had the distinct impression that the Howe women looked down on me. They certainly addressed me with distaste, and I them.

Mr. Aganos admired me for my drive to learn and certainly wanted to help me; but he lost his patience with me when I constantly contradicted and argued with him, my teachers, and fellow students. He got very tired of my misbehavior and on several occasions threatened to expel me. However, in spite of all of our problems, we were to remain friends for years to come.

Soon it was graduation year.

*   *   *

As graduation ceremonies for the class of 1886 were approaching, I was named valedictorian of my class of eight students and asked to make an address at the commencement exercises. I was excited about this opportunity and worked late into the nights preparing my talk. I loved words. It was certainly not a chore for me to write my speech.

I was concerned about what I would wear to the ceremonies. I had nothing but the secondhand dresses I had been given over the years, old shoes, worn stockings, and no money to buy clothes. Two weeks before graduation, my dear Mrs. Hopkins presented me with a beautiful new white lace dress she had made and new white shoes and stockings. There was a pink ribbon at the waistline of the dress. I was delighted. I had never had new clothes before. Every night I took the dress out of my closet and held it up to me to admire in the mirror and dusted the shiny new shoes.

June 1 finally came, and wearing my new outfit with my hair piled in neat curls high on my head, I confidently approached the podium to give my commencement speech. Just prior to the commencement ceremony, my favorite teacher, Miss Moore, pinned a corsage of beautiful pink miniature roses to my dress. For the first time in my life, I felt truly beautiful.

Ceremonies were held at Tremont Temple in Boston. There was loud applause when I finished my speech. It received rave reviews in all of the local papers. What an exciting day it was. I had achieved my lifelong goal to learn to read and much more. My hard work had paid off. I couldn't possibly thank Miss Moore, all of the other teachers who patiently taught me, Mrs. Hopkins, and especially Mr. Aganos enough!

After all of the speeches were over and diplomas presented, there was a celebration party with delicious finger sandwiches, an assortment of sweets, and tea. Exhausted from the excitement of the day, Mrs. Hopkins and I went back to the school to retrieve our belongings and travel to Cape Cod for the summer. Before we left, I took a long walk through the halls of this wonderful school and paused in various classrooms to lovingly touch the desks where I had spent many hours. I realized I would probably never be there again. What a difference this place made to my life. Maggie Carroll would be so proud of me now. I shall have to get word to her at Tewksbury.

I was twenty years old, and I had been at Perkins for six years.

16

TUSCUMBIA, ALABAMA

Settled in for the summer at Cape Cod, I worried over what I would do with my life now. Mr. Aganos and I had discussed my prospects, and they weren't very good. I needed to have more schooling to become a teacher, and funds weren't available. I certainly didn't want to become a housemaid or perform dull tasks for some manufacturer for the rest of my life.

Mrs. Hopkins kindly told me to take my time over the summer to figure it out. What a dear she was. By the end of the summer, no opportunities for employment had come my way. I was becoming a little desperate. I couldn't live the rest of my life with Mrs. Hopkins. I had to earn a living.

I took long walks along the beach every day, thinking about my prospects. Had I not had that beautiful summer in Cape Cod with Mrs. Hopkins, I would have gone mad with worry about my future. When I fretted, she gave me hope. Just having her as my friend made the worries easier to bear.

Toward the end of the summer, I was having problems with my eyes again. They felt like they were full of sand and were red and sore. A subsequent visit to Dr. Bradford revealed that I had granules on my eyes and lids. Fortunately there was a new drug called Jequirity made of scarlet and black beans and water. It had been found to work very well to resolve this problem in other patients.

On September 1, I was admitted to the Carney Catholic Hospital, and a solution of this drug was administered to my eyes several times a day for seventeen days. Success again! I actually had slight improvement in my vision.

*   *   *

Soon after I returned from the hospital to Cape Cod, I received a letter from Mr. Aganos asking if I was interested in moving to Tuscumbia, Alabama, to teach a blind/deaf seven-year-old girl. Her father had consulted with educator Dr. Alexander Graham Bell who advised him to seek a teacher for his daughter from Perkins Institute for the Blind. I would receive room and board plus twenty-five dollars a month.

I was thrilled to finally have the offer of a position but unsure whether I was qualified for such an undertaking. In addition, I had never been out of Massachusetts and a little anxious about moving so far away. However, I knew I had no other options and advised Mr. Aganos that I would indeed take the job. I requested time to do research at Perkins before I left. Mr. Aganos was very helpful. He was excited for me and made me to promise to send him regular reports of my progress.

I went back to Perkins and began going through all of the documentation of Dr. Howe's teaching methods of Laura Bridgman. Fortunately, I already knew how he communicated with her through hand fingering from the time I spent with her as her roommate. I pored over his documentation until my eyes forced me to rest.

One thing that I definitely wanted to do differently with my little ward was teach her to be as independent as possible. I also wanted her to learn to play and not be confined inside. She had to be able to leave her home. But first of course, I must meet this child and determine her capabilities.

Before my journey, I made another visit to Dr. Bradford. I had another minor surgery to correct a mild cross-eye and was released with a good bill of health.

I said a tearful goodbye to my friend Mrs. Hopkins. How I would miss her! She had taught me kindness through her kindness and love through her love. After promises to write often, I was off on my journey to Tuscumbia, Alabama, to meet little Helen Keller.

*   *   *

I left Perkins with a doll for Helen from the students, a dress for the doll made by Laura Bridgman, money, and a garnet ring from Mr. Aganos.

One of the teachers accompanied me to the train station. It was March 1887, and I was twenty years old.

Unfortunately the trip took much longer than expected. I had to change trains several times and finally arrived in Washington, D.C., to find that I had missed my train to Tuscumbia and had to wait until the following morning to continue my long journey. I panicked. Fortunately, a friend of Mr. Aganos's had met me at the train station, and he arranged for me to stay at a hotel for the night. I wouldn't have had the faintest idea how to get to or check into a hotel.

By the time I got to my room, my eyes hurt, my feet were swollen from the unfamiliar shoes I was wearing, and I was exhausted. After soaking my feet in cool water, I got into bed and cried, yearning to go back to Mrs. Hopkins in Cape Cod and my familiar bed. I was uncertain if I had made a wise decision to commit to this teaching job. I was traveling for the first time by myself, going to a faraway, strange place to live, and undertaking a job I was not sure I could handle. I certainly didn't enjoy my first night in a hotel.

The following day, on March 3, 1887, I arrived in Tuscumbia, Alabama, tired, disheveled, with red, swollen, sore eyes. I hadn't been able to get shoes on my swollen feet and was forced to wear slippers. Everyone looked at my feet, and I wondered at the first impression I would make on the Keller family.

I got off the train and was met by Mrs. Keller and her stepson James. Mrs. Keller was much younger than I expected. Later I found out that she had married Captain Keller when she was twenty-two years old and he was forty-two years old. He had been married before and been widowed with two sons.

Kate Keller was tall and stately with fair skin and blue eyes. Her stepson James was dark with a large build. He was surly and didn't speak other than to shake my hand and say hello. He was probably about my age.

Of course their eyes were immediately drawn to my feet. I made an embarrassed apology about my slippers and described my exhausting trip from Boston to Tuscumbia. I was certainly glad my journey was over.

On our way to her home, Mrs. Keller painfully described the situation with her seven-year-old daughter, Helen. It was obvious to me that it was a difficult subject for her to share.

Helen had been ill with a high fever when she was nineteen months old and ever since then had been blind and deaf. She used a few hand signals to communicate her needs but didn't attempt to talk. She had known several words and sentences before her illness. Helen had been a delightful, happy baby. Since her illness, all laughter and expression was gone. She was unresponsive and as she got older had become very difficult to manage. She refused to have her hair washed and combed, and it was nearly impossible to dress her. She had grown big enough that it wasn't easy to physically restrain her to bathe or dress her. They were desperate for help.

From her voice and expression, it was obvious Mrs. Keller loved Helen dearly and suffered over her inability to teach and nurture her daughter.

I told Mrs. Keller that it was very fortunate that Helen was nineteen months old before she lost her sight. Children blind since birth have to be taught to crawl and walk since they can't imitate. They don't realize they are separate from everything around them. They have no sense of self. Fortunately Helen could navigate and had experienced light and sound. She knew she was an individual. Her training would go much faster without having to take the time to teach her essential things that children blind at birth must learn.

We finally turned up a shady lane edged by beautiful large English boxwood trees. At the end of the lane stood the Keller home, Ivy Green, obviously named so because of the English ivy that surrounded the house, covering the fences and trees. It was a large white house. Beautiful large trees and bushes I had never seen before were everywhere.

I noticed a separate little house just to the right of the main house on the other side of the pump, which looked vacant. I found out later it had previously been used for an office. Behind the house were separate buildings where the servants lived and the horses were stabled. I was appalled that they had slaves. There was a large kitchen in one of the buildings where meals were prepared and several outbuildings and a large barn.

Captain Arthur Keller came out to greet us and help us out of the carriage. He was a nice-looking tall large-built man with piercing blue eyes. His son James looked a great deal like him. Captain Keller had fought with the Confederate army and had owned and been editor of the *North Alabamian* weekly newspaper. He also was U.S. marshal for the Northern District of Alabama for President Grover Cleveland. He considered himself a gentleman farmer. I was to find later that he did not have a good business head and struggled to maintain Ivy Green.

A disheveled little girl stood on the porch, her chestnut brown hair uncombed and hanging in her face, wearing a rumpled, dirty dress. She looked healthy and had a pretty but expressionless face. I was immediately drawn to her.

Helen detected her mother was there and anxiously extended her arms. Instead, I took her hands and reached down to kiss her. When she realized I was not her mother, she pulled away from me and frantically tried to find her mother. Once she received reassurance from her mother that all was well, she cautiously approached me and then suddenly searched around with her hands and finding my bag, grabbed it and tried to open it. Embarrassed at her behavior, Mrs. Keller pulled her away; and as she did, Helen started kicking and hitting her. The maid, who was introduced to me later as Ella, ran over and helped restrain Helen until she calmed down. Helen acted like an angry, wild little animal.

As I gazed at that child, I certainly understood the fear, anger, and frustration she felt. Oh, how much I understood. My heart ached for her. It was like looking back in time at my own feelings when I was six and lost my sight. She did not understand what had happened to her. She was living in darkness as well as silence. No wonder she was frightened and angry.

Somehow I managed to get her attention and show her my watch. She ran her hands over it and then reached up and touched my face. When I followed James as he carried my bags into the house and up to my room, Helen curiously followed. James set my bags down, looked at Helen with what I thought was disgust, wished me good luck, and left. Helen began feeling around and found my bag, opened it, and started pulling things out.

She had none of the nervous habits that many blind children have. We wouldn't have to deal with her swaying her head back and forth, rubbing and gouging her eyes, running her hands over everything, and pacing. However, it was obvious she was a headstrong little girl who was totally undisciplined. I had a big job ahead of me.

When suppertime came, I was famished. Ella served a delicious meal of roasted chicken, potatoes and gravy, home-canned green beans, fresh bread, and of course grits. I thought grits looked more like a breakfast dish but found that they were quite delicious for supper with butter and salt and pepper. The meal was topped with vanilla custard and chocolate cake.

I was shocked that Helen was allowed to go from her father and mother and grab food off their plates with her hand and stuff it in her mouth. She didn't attempt to take food from James. I would guess he had shooed her away enough to discourage her. Food was all over the floor and many times on everyone else. They just ignored her eating habits. When I didn't let her take the food off my plate, she went into a wild rage, grabbing and throwing everything she found within her reach. Captain and Mrs. Keller hurried and explained that she just wanted something to eat. I told them she should be sitting at the table eating like everyone else. It was obvious they were disturbed, and the meal ended quickly. James gave me a nod of approval.

After supper I excused myself and went straight to my room. I was very weary and tired from the long day of traveling and the emotional strain of my first few hours at the Kellers'. I climbed gratefully into my warm, clean bed and thought about my little charge. Before I could teach her anything, I had to get her attention, and she would have to be disciplined. I fell asleep while pondering this.

*   *   *

After a good night's rest, I awoke early, refreshed and anxious to begin my work with little Helen. Ella showed me to the dining room where a hearty breakfast of eggs, sausages, toast, and grits awaited me. I had slept a little later than I had planned, and the rest of the family had already eaten. Ella explained that they didn't want to disturb me and thought I might need extra rest after my trip. I certainly appreciated the extra hour of rest.

Ella left me to my breakfast, and soon Mrs. Keller brought Helen in to me. She clung to her mother's skirts until she smelled the food. She darted straight to the sideboard and started grabbing food and stuffing it in her mouth. A big portion of it went on the floor. Once again, there was no attempt to stop her.

I had decided to start teaching Helen by fingerspelling words the way Dr. Howe had taught Laura Bridgman.

I persuaded Helen to follow me up to my room and let her rummage through my trunk until she found the doll the children at Perkins had sent her. When she picked it up, I took her hand and spelled the word D-O-L-L into it. She thought I was taking the doll away from her and immediately started kicking her feet and pushing me away. After she calmed down, we went downstairs; and since she seemed to enjoy food so much, I gave her a piece of cake and then spelled the word C-A-K-E in her hand. She repeated the movement in my hand, but I knew she didn't have the faintest idea what it meant.

She was curious and willing to follow me around. We touched items around the house and spelled their names back and forth to each other. Even though she fingerspelled the names back to me, I knew she had no comprehension of what they meant. It was just a game to her.

Over the next several days, I was amazed when I saw what Helen had taught herself over the last five years. She had remembered from her infancy yes and no by shaking her head. Pulling on her mother meant "come" and pushing meant "go." These signs were understandable, but I was stunned when she went to the ice chest and stood there shaking, and Mrs. Keller explained to me that it meant she wanted her to make ice cream for dinner! Helen could fold clothes and put them away, knowing which ones were hers.

She played outside with Ella's daughter Martha who was about her age. Helen was entirely in charge of these playtimes, and if Ella didn't follow exactly what she wanted, Helen would lose her temper and start hitting her. Ella seemed to understand and gave in to all of Helen's desires.

Together they fed the chickens and turkeys, gathered eggs, and helped with kitchen chores. During milking time, Helen stood with her arms around the cow, feeling its life and warmth. All of this behavior was achieved on her own with no direction.

She seemed to only be happy when she was busy. This was not surprising to me because if she wasn't busy, she only knew darkness and silence. Helen could communicate in these small ways to others but couldn't understand anything others tried to tell or teach her. She had managed to learn as much as she could by herself and yearned to learn more and be like the people who surrounded her.

At her age, she was bound to understand that she was different and couldn't do what others did. This was probably the reason that her temper and anger had steadily grown worse as she got older.

If she didn't get her way, she kicked and screamed until she got it. When she had a temper tantrum, the family used food, mostly cake, to quiet her. That was the extent of her two-way communication.

Her lack of table manners bothered me most of all. When she came to my plate, I never let her touch my food. She hit and thrashed around and several times pulled plates off the table and threw them on the floor. The family got upset with me for not giving in to her, but I insisted that she could learn to eat like everyone else.

Finally, after a very unsettling, stressful meal, I begged the family to leave so I could work with Helen alone on table etiquette. With great reluctance, they left me alone with Helen, and I locked the door.

Several hours later, the room was in total disarray with food and broken dishes everywhere, but I had succeeded in getting Helen to eat at the table with a fork from a plate. She even learned to sit with a napkin on her lap. How obstinate she had been! Both Helen and I left the dining room completely exhausted and covered in food. I reported to an anxious Mrs. Keller that Helen could now sit and eat with the family properly.

Mrs. Keller led Helen away to clean her up, and I went to my room to change and take a nap. I was totally exhausted and knew Helen was also. At supper after a few reminders, Helen sat at the table and ate like a human being. Needless to say, the Kellers were very shocked and pleased.

As the days passed, I found it difficult to work with Helen when her family was present. She had been allowed to do as she pleased for so long that she refused to do anything for me. They always made allowances for her actions and came to her defense when they felt I was too harsh. She knew if she threw temper tantrums the family would immediately calm her down with cake. They rewarded her for bad behavior. Frustrated, I finally told them that the only way we would make progress would be if Helen and I were by ourselves. Both Captain and Mrs. Keller strongly objected.

I kept insisting that a period of isolation was the only way we could ever continue with Helen's training. They finally relented, and we arranged to stay in the small cottage next to the house with a servant child who would run errands for me. We agreed that they could come and see Helen every day but could not let her know they were there. They had to stay outside and look through the window. Helen was driven around in a carriage and returned to the cottage later in the day. She didn't know where she was and had no idea she was right next door to her home.

When she was ushered into the cottage, I was waiting for her. As the door was closed and locked behind her, she ran and started pounding and kicking it. Somehow she seemed to sense what was happening. Every time I approached her, she kicked at me and then turned her back to me. Finally she wore herself out and slumped down on the floor beside the door. Supper came, and I was happy to see her eat well, sitting nicely at the table. Immediately after she finished eating, she sat on the floor and played with her doll until it was bedtime, totally ignoring me.

I handed her a nightgown. She put it on by herself and then climbed into bed. But as soon as I slipped in beside her, she scrambled out of bed and refused to lie back down. For two hours I fought with her trying to get her in bed. Every time she got up, I wrestled her back into the bed. Finally, exhausted, she let me put her in the bed; and I crawled in beside her. We both immediately fell asleep.

The battle of wills continued with a near failure when the Kellers decided they couldn't stand their little girl so unhappy and felt that I was mistreating her. After arguing and pleading, I persuaded them that it was the only way to teach her the discipline required to proceed with any further training. Their only other option was to let her remain the way she was.

They reluctantly agreed, and in two weeks' time I was able to tame Helen, and the tantrums ended. I was even able to clean her up and fix her hair. It's a good thing because I don't know how much longer I could have tolerated our situation. You may ask how I did it. With a firm hand, privileges given and privileges taken away. I didn't want to break her spirit, but she had to learn that her behavior was unacceptable. I spent many nights lying awake analyzing what worked and what didn't.

17

THE BREAKTHROUGH

It was nearly spring, my favorite time of year, and we began spending most of our time out-of-doors. I introduced Helen to the names of trees, flowers, the dirt, and grass. Everything within our reach that we touched I spelled. We smelled the wonderful fragrance of the yellow jasmine and found little white mayapples hiding under their leaves beneath the large trees in the yard. We admired the delicate trout lily that only opens and shows her face during the day and closes her beautiful petals at night to rest. Helen loved the feeling and smell of the spring wildflowers we found in the meadow.

Around the house, the fragrant red, yellow, and white roses, coral honeysuckle, and red-berried smilax were just beginning to bloom. English ivy lay in thick carpets on the ground and wound and curled itself over fences and up around trees. We examined all of these wonders, but still Helen didn't associate the words I was spelling in her hand to the object. I know she was bursting to be able to "talk" about her feelings for everything she was experiencing. I kept spelling and spelling in an attempt to give her words.

Our big day came when I was spelling M-U-G to her as she held a mug of water. She got mug and water confused. After several attempts to identify these objects separately, I took her outside to the pump and put her hand with the mug underneath the flowing water. As the water spilled out of the mug onto her hand, I again spelled W-A-T-E-R. Then I put her hand without the mug under the flowing water and spelled W-A-T-E-R again. She paused a moment and excitedly put her hand in the water and spelled into my hand W-A-T-E-R. Success!

I wept with joy as I hugged her and called to the family to come see what she knew. We had finally broken through the darkness, and Helen would now be able to learn words and communicate. She immediately threw herself down on the ground and touched the grass holding up her hand for me to spell the word for grass. The family stood spellbound as they watched us scramble from tree, to bush, to flower as I spelled words to Helen.

Helen and I revisited all of the beautiful spring flowers, and she learned their names. I followed her around the yard for the rest of the day spelling the words of various objects into her hands. We were both exhausted by suppertime. We had a joyous celebration at supper that evening. Ella baked Helen's favorite rich chocolate cake.

I was very tired, but my elation over our breakthrough kept me from falling asleep that night. That was one of the most joyous days of my life.

*   *   *

By the end of June, four months after I started working with Helen, she knew four hundred words. After she realized what words meant, I started teaching her how to read raised-dot print letters and copy the letters on paper using a grooved board I had brought with me from Perkins.

She still did not have any concept of sentences. I thought about how sighted and hearing children learned to talk and realized Helen had to be taught the same way. I started talking sentences to Helen the same way infants are spoken to. In time, I introduced adjectives and verbs and then started putting them all together. I knew I was successful when Helen began asking for descriptions of objects.

We also started working on arithmetic, counting little wooden beads and straws. Helen hated it but soon had mastered addition and subtraction.

Our out-of-doors classroom became much more exciting for Helen now that she could communicate. She could describe the pretty soft flower, the cool damp grass, the flutter of air from a dragonfly's wings, and the warm sun in the blue sky. She felt the softness of new leaves and ran her fingers over their life-providing veins. Sometimes the leaves were wet with dew, and I had to explain the difference between rain and dew. Every day we wandered around Ivy Green, and I painstakingly explained every detail of our little world.

Helen demanded to be talked to from the time she got up in the morning until she went to bed at night. She was pale and exhausted and grew fussy easily. The family was alarmed at Helen's deteriorating health and called in the doctor. He said she was suffering from fatigue. They told me I was pushing Helen too hard, but then after we discussed our daily routine, they agreed that Helen was driving our breakneck speed.

We were both exhausted. My eyes were so tired I suffered from nausea and headaches. Fatigued, I lost my patience and courage and became discontent. Tiredness weakened my ability to focus. Many nights my restless sleep was interrupted by memories from my childhood, and I awoke frightened and sobbing. I was plagued by dreams that I was still at Tewksbury and relived some of the horrors I had experienced there.

Mrs. Keller and I decided to encourage Helen to take a nap every day after lunch. This was welcoming news to me. I was able to rest my eyes and fingers and prepare for the rigorous activities of the afternoon. After our noon meals, I spread a blanket on the ground under one of the magnolia trees or lay cushions on the porch and spelled stories in her hand until she fell asleep. I got a much-needed rest as well. She usually woke up first and shook me awake to continue her adventures into awareness.

One of my most rewarding accomplishments that first year was teaching Helen how to laugh. We had played and run outside, made mud cakes, and romped with her dog Belle; but throughout this time she never really laughed like little girls do.

One morning I went into her room laughing and put her hands on my face to feel the vibration of the laughter and see how my face contorted. Then I showed her how to tickle me and make me laugh, and then I tickled her until she laughed. To the delight of everyone, her laughter was soon heard throughout the house.

As her communication advanced, so did her sensory perceptions. Amazingly she could soon tell the color of a flower by touch and smell. She knew when it was going to rain.

She was excited and surprisingly gentle when she held a baby chick. She smelled it and caressed its soft down. She was given a piglet to hold and screeched with delight as it wiggled and snorted trying to get back to its brothers and sisters. We explored the different textures of leaves from the various trees in the yard and compared them to leaves of vegetables and flowers in the garden.

Hours were spent along the Tennessee River at Keller's landing playing in the mud and discovering what was buried there. She felt the sensation of mud oozing up between her toes and held a wiggly worm in her hand and felt the softness of its skin. I taught her geography by building mountains and cities out of mud.

Each day as Helen became more aware of her world, her face shone with happiness. Captain and Mrs. Keller were ecstatic over the progress we had made. Over the months there had been lots of concern and doubt regarding my teaching methods, and on several occasions our arguments nearly ended in the severing of our relationship. I stubbornly refused to consider changing what I was doing. I had no doubt in my mind that I perceived what Helen needed. The only reason they allowed me to continue was because of Helen's progress and the close relationship that had developed between us.

Neither Captain nor Mrs. Keller could fingerspell to Helen. I sensed that Mrs. Keller was bothered and perhaps jealous of the relationship developing between Helen and me. Helen was with me from sunup to sundown and spent very little time with her mother.

Fearing that she may become distressed enough to hamper our progress, I suggested she learn our finger language. Her communication skills with Helen were always limited, and I know she always resented my close relationship with her daughter. I believe Mrs. Keller loved Helen so much that she accepted her loss so Helen could be taught to live her life to its fullness. She knew she was not capable of teaching her. Fortunately, she had Helen's little sister Mildred.

We never really talked or became friends until Helen was an adult. You would think that living under the same roof we would have gotten to know each other. That was not the case.

Ivy Green was not a comfortable household in which to live. I enjoyed having my own tidy room, but the rest of the house was in disarray. I have always detested untidiness, probably because I lived in such filth as a child. I also hated the living conditions of the servants and the way they were treated.

However, Ella, the maid, seemed happy and was a very good cook. I certainly enjoyed Southern cooking. In addition to the food, I marveled at the beauty of the country. There was such a beautiful array of color. The flowers were abundant and stood out against the green of the thick foliage like beacons on a dark night.

Captain Keller ignored me and had the typical Southern gentlemen's superior attitude toward women. His son James was only seen at mealtimes and spent the rest of his time overseeing the work of the slaves. I must say, though, that they made it very clear to me on several occasions how grateful they were that I had come into their lives and done so much for Helen.

The few conversations I had with the family and their guests usually ended with me expressing my distaste for the South's political views and despicable use of slaves. I couldn't help myself. Soon, mealtimes were limited to polite conversation, and it was evident that everyone avoided talk of politics when I was around. I didn't really mind because most of my attention was on Helen. I never really had any other friends there.

Sometimes I was lonely and wished for adult conversation, but I buried those feelings and basked in the love of Helen.

I continued to expose Helen to everything possible that other children experienced. She stood with her hands on the piano feeling the vibrations as I played, and she learned about music. When Mrs. Keller played the piano, Helen and I danced to the vibration of the music.

She soon was able to identify everyone in the household by the vibration of their step. I could call her by tapping my foot on the floor, and she would sense it and come to me. The pace of her learning and understanding was unbelievable.

I don't know that she was necessarily brighter than other children. When you spend every waking moment with a blind/deaf child who cannot be distracted by other activities or noises, they are bound to learn much quicker and absorb more than sighted and hearing children.

Before I left Perkins, I had agreed to write regular reports to Mr. Aganos at Perkins telling him about our progress and breakthroughs. Mr. Aganos was skeptical about the accuracy of the reports I was giving him and made a trip from Boston to Tuscumbia to see Helen for himself. He was charmed by this little girl and amazed at what she had learned. When he returned to Boston, Helen wrote him letters regularly.

Dr. Alexander Graham Bell also got regular reports. Both men were delighted with what they heard, and it wasn't long before the story of Helen Keller was told around the world. She became famous, and our world changed drastically. We were always being hounded for interviews and photographs for newspapers and magazines. The Kellers and I had to fight to keep our privacy.

*   *   *

Dr. Alexander Graham Bell loved Helen and was extremely interested in the development of her communication skills. He became a welcome, regular visitor to Tuscumbia. He was very supportive of me and constantly gave me compliments about my work. I felt very honored to be the recipient of his compliments. He praised me to the newspapers and in the articles he published.

Dr. Bell was thrilled at Helen's progress. He was very interested in working with the deaf. His mother and wife were both deaf.

He had won the French government's Volta Prize of fifty thousand dollars in 1879 for his invention of the telephone. Bell used this money to establish the Volta Associates where research of recording and transmitting sound was done. Proceeds from patents of the gramophone developed by the Volta Association were used to found the Volta Bureau. The Volta

Bureau worked closely with the American Association for the Promotion of the Teaching of Speech to the Deaf.

We became good friends and were close until his death in 1922. He was the only one that stood behind me through tumultuous times, encouraged me when I became fearful, and praised me for my accomplishments. I was always at ease with him. Over the years, we spent many happy days with the Bell family, and his daughter Daisy and Helen became the best of friends. They were about the same age.

Sometimes when he visited, he brought along Mr. Hitz, his secretary. He was an older gentleman whom I came to look upon as a father figure. We wrote to each other regularly.

18

BOSTON

While Mr. Aganos was visiting us at Ivy Green during the summer of 1887, I begged him to let us come to Perkins for a while. I was tired of the monotony in Alabama and thought it would do both Helen and me good to spend time at Perkins. In November, we received a welcome letter from him inviting Helen, Mrs. Keller, and me to spend several months in Boston. I was very happy to get out of the South for a while.

We arrived at Mr. Aganos's home in Boston the end of May 1888 and attended the Perkins commencement ceremonies where Helen was asked to read a poem. Everyone adored the beautiful seven-year-old blind/deaf child that confidently got on stage and read a poem with one hand and signed what she read to me to repeat to the audience. It appeared to me that most of the people there were more interested in Helen than the commencement ceremony.

Mrs. Howe was not at the ceremony. I was sure it was because she thought I was trying to denigrate her late husband's accomplishments with Laura Bridgman. I had already surpassed what he had accomplished with Laura. She had made several derogatory remarks to me about my skills as a teacher in front of a group of people earlier in the week. We were always enemies and never had any respect for each other.

Helen, Mrs. Keller, and I spent the entire summer with my dear Mrs. Hopkins in Cape Cod. It was wonderful to be back in the Boston area, but

I was unnerved at the numerous invitations we received to attend various functions and dinners. I had always been an outcast and looked down upon by the same people that now wanted to be my friend, so I would parade Helen around at their functions. We attended only those I felt we needed to attend, which in my mind were too many!

Mr. Aganos was with us as much as possible. He and Helen were very close and enjoyed each other's company. He was lonely from being recently widowed and seemed to enjoy my companionship as well. I begged him to attend many of the functions with us because he knew how difficult they were for me. He graciously escorted me to many of these events, and some people actually thought we were a couple.

We met some wonderful people while we were in Boston. Poets Oliver Wendell Holmes and John Greenleaf Whittier delighted Helen with their poems. She wrote to them regularly and sent them poems she had written herself. The poems of John Greenleaf Whittier touched her deeply with his descriptions of flowers, birds, and people.

Helen had no idea I was miserable, and she had a wonderful summer. I introduced her to the ocean, and she loved the cold salty ocean water, after the initial shock of feeling its power. The summer and fall passed quickly, and by December we were back in Tuscumbia. We brought back lots of books for Helen's further study.

I introduced Helen to more advanced arithmetic and reading as well as zoology.

*   *   *

My eyes started bothering me a great deal, and I realized I must see Dr. Bradford again. My sight was blurry, and my eyes were red and sore. I arranged with Captain and Mrs. Keller to take a leave of absence from June through October 1889 to return to Boston for treatment. Eva Ramsdell, a student at Perkins, was scheduled to go to Tuscumbia and be a companion for Helen while I was gone.

It was the first time in three years that my darling Helen and I would be separated. I knew it would be hard on Helen, and I certainly would miss that child! Oh, how I had grown to love her.

*   *   *

While I was resting my eyes, I gave a lot of thought to how I would proceed with Helen's education. I realized that I had taught her as much as I could at Ivy Green. We needed more books, additional classes that I wasn't qualified to teach, and interaction with other children.

I wrote to our dear friend Mr. Aganos, director of Perkins Institute for the Blind, asking that ten-year-old Helen and I be allowed to continue her studies at Perkins. We had no funds and would have to be able to attend without expense to the Kellers. He was in Europe at the time, and his assistant John A. Bennett took the matter under consideration. After waiting for several long weeks, I received a letter from Mr. Bennett advising me that Helen and I would be most welcome.

We soon found ourselves in Boston. It was wonderful to be back at my old school. I was exhilarated when I saw the brilliant color of the fall trees and felt the cool breeze that hinted of the coming winter. How I loved the clean, crisp air of fall! As we entered the school, we walked through crispy fallen leaves that crackled under our feet with each step. Here I was again, entering Perkins at a different time in my life with a new little student named Helen.

I remained Helen's primary teacher; and we began studying advanced arithmetic, geography, form, and zoology. With other teachers at the school, Helen studied basketry, clay modeling, music, and French. I attended all of these classes with Helen to spell the lectures and instructions to her. Miss Marrett was Helen's French teacher. She was convinced Helen had a photographic mind. She remembered everything and never needed review.

Within three months, Helen was able to write a long letter in French to Mr. Aganos. She continued to correspond regularly with Dr. Alexander Graham Bell, Oliver Wendell Holmes, and John Greenleaf Whittier. I was so proud her.

During the first few months at Perkins, Helen learned of a blind/deaf girl in Norway who had learned to speak. I did not want Helen to pursue speaking because I was certain it would distract from her studies and also knew that most deaf people's speech was unintelligible.

Helen persisted, and I finally gave in and took her to a speech therapist by the name of Mrs. Fuller. She placed Helen's hand on her face and the fingers of her other hand in her mouth so Helen could learn the vibration of speech and the position of the tongue. She practiced on me until I gagged. It was during these exercises that Helen learned to read people's speech by placing her forefinger on their lips and thumb on their throat. She used this method her entire life.

Mr. Aganos wrote in his next report that Helen had learned to speak in two months. Unfortunately this was not really true. The only people who could understand her were Mrs. Fuller and me. Speech became a regular part of our studies, but Helen was extremely disappointed that only a few people could understand her. Her vocal cords had not developed, and she was never able to speak clearly.

Helen became very popular with the Boston elite, and we were invited to many of their parties. However, through their actions and words, it was obvious to me that they were only interested in Helen. Many times they actually had their backs turned to me while they fussed over Helen. I was treated as though I were a servant. I was extremely uncomfortable at these events. They looked down on me. When they did feel they had a duty to speak to me, they were condescending. I hated it and found myself making offensive remarks in response. I intentionally offended them. I turned down several invitations because I was so uncomfortable in their presence.

Unfortunately I also had problems with the teachers at Perkins. They seemed to resent the fact that I insisted on teaching most subjects to Helen myself. They also didn't like the fact that we were treated as guests of the school. We came and went as we pleased and didn't follow their strict rules and regulations. Conversations with the teachers were limited. I resented any of their comments or recommendations regarding Helen's curriculum. I knew what I was doing and didn't want any interference.

Mr. Aganos wrote an article for the local paper that insinuated Helen's early educational methods had been developed by the school's first director, Dr. Howe, and she had continued most of her education at Perkins. I took this to mean that Perkins teachers taught Helen. I was furious that they were obviously using Helen for publicity for the school. It ended our year at Perkins on a sour note when I declared in an interview for the newspaper that Helen was not educated by Perkins but by me. We merely used the facilities and equipment of the school. I also made my feelings clear about the Boston elite.

Helen had been scheduled to speak at the commencement exercises but was removed from the program by the board of directors. We did not even attend the ceremonies. We had been at Perkins for eight months, and I knew Helen needed more time to study there. I realized I had made a grave mistake by alienating the teachers and directors and immediately sent letters of apology to the Perkins board and a separate letter to Mr. Aganos. I certainly didn't want to hurt our chances of returning to Perkins in the fall.

*   *   *

We spent our first week of summer vacation with William Wade, a philanthropist who lived in Hulton, Pennsylvania. He was very supportive of education for the blind and deaf. He adored Helen and had purchased her a new donkey named Neddy and a bullmastiff named Lioness. He was very generous with his support of us, and it was important I maintain our relationship.

After leaving the Wades, we had a pleasant visit with Dr. Alexander Graham Bell's family on their farm with the usual picnics, boat trips on the river, and, to my delight, horseback riding. Helen and I both loved horses and were thrilled when we got a chance to ride. I always rode on a horse ahead of Helen, leading her horse. Dr. Bell's assistant, Mr. Hitz, visited often. He loved Helen dearly and showed a great deal of fondness for me also.

The last weeks of summer were spent in Tuscumbia. Fall soon arrived, and we returned to school in Boston.

*   *   *

Helen was eleven years old when we returned to Perkins in the fall of 1891. Mr. Aganos's birthday was approaching, and Helen had spent the summer writing a book for him. She named it *The Frost King*. On his birthday, she proudly presented him with the book, and he was delighted. He was so taken with her story that he had it printed in several magazines.

Soon after the story was published, Mr. Aganos was notified that the story had already been written by Margaret T. Canby and published in her book *Birdie and His Fairy Friends*. He called Helen into his office and asked her, through another interpreter, about the story. I was not allowed to attend.

Helen truly believed that she had made up the story herself. I found out from Mrs. Hopkins that the book was at her house, and we probably had read it to her over the summer. I immediately wrote a letter explaining that we indeed had no memory of reading Margaret Canby's story, but it may have been read to her over the summer a few years before. The matter seemed to be dropped.

Then, to my horror, Helen told one of the teachers I had read her the story last fall. I was disliked by the teacher, so she was thrilled to report the conversation she had with Helen to Mr. Aganos. This forced him to call for a full investigation. Thankfully, he did not blame Helen for anything. All blame was placed on me. Yes, I may have read her the book. I didn't really remember. I had made a grave error by not admitting I was unsure whether I had read her the story or not. I didn't even know what plagiarism was or I may have paid more attention.

The investigation was extremely painful for us but especially for my innocent little Helen. She had just turned twelve years old. I had sheltered her so much over the years from any negative situations that she had never experienced suspicion or distrust. She was very frightened and confused by the harshness of the investigators' questions.

The investigators voted, and it was a tie. Mr. Aganos was the tiebreaker and voted in Helen's favor. The issue was over. However, Mr. Aganos never trusted me again. I was deeply hurt and would truly miss him as a good friend. We had become very close. I had made many enemies at Perkins. Mrs. Howe, the teachers, and now added to the list, the Perkins Board of Directors and Mr. Aganos. It pained me to see Helen suffer with the loss of his friendship. She wrote him several letters telling him she missed him and got no response. In time, he started writing back to her, but it was too late. He had already wounded her deeply.

By the time *The Frost King* incident was over, it was the end of the school year, and we returned to Tuscumbia. I was very relieved to get away from Boston and the dark clouds that hung over us there.

19

DESPERATION, 1892

With *The Frost King* incident behind us, we returned to Tuscumbia where a troubled Captain and Mrs. Keller awaited us. Everything was in turmoil at Ivy Green. Four years earlier, Captain Keller had lost his government position as U.S. marshal after Republican Benjamin Harrison defeated Democrat Grover Cleveland and won the 1888 presidential election.

There was no money. Captain Keller had gone through all of their savings, and everything he owned was mortgaged. He had demanded all funds sent to Perkins for Helen be under his control, and he spent it. He was desperate and tried everything to get funds, even using his daughter Helen and me.

Captain Keller had nearly been successful a few years earlier putting Helen on show in vaudeville, but Mrs. Keller immediately had put a stop to that idea. Now, he was approaching the people who had contributed to Helen and my expenses for loans. Every dime contributed for our support he continued to spend. I had not been paid for two years.

When we arrived at Ivy Green, we discovered that baby Phillip had whooping cough and James typhoid fever. Mrs. Keller was exhausted. There was no one to help her, and I had to immediately roll up my sleeves and relieve her of the household duties. Mrs. Keller did the nursing. It was miserably hot and humid, and it took every ounce of energy we had to make it through the day. Our clothes clung to us, wet with perspiration.

Because of the heat, no one rested well at night. The mattresses seemed to have absorbed and held the heat of the day.

I hung cold wet cloths throughout the downstairs to cool down the rooms, but they did little to relieve the stifling heat and only added to the humidity. We all slept in various places downstairs because the heat in the upstairs bedrooms was unbearable. I kept Helen far away from the sick boys and occupied her as best I could with little chores she could do.

When the heat wave finally broke and Phillip and James had recovered enough, the family moved to Fern Quarry, a small house the Kellers owned in the mountains. You could hardly call it a house. It was small, very rustic, and dirty. Spiders had spun their webs in every corner. I could hardly see out of the dirty windows. The floors were covered with a thick film of dust and dirt, and rugs and cushions had to be aired before we could use them. We spent the first week cleaning and making it livable. At least it was cooler there, but we didn't have a cook or a nurse and were a mile from any neighbor. Captain Keller didn't help at all and feigned business to return to Tuscumbia.

Helen was so despondent over *The Frost King* incident that we suspended all studying for the summer. I became very concerned about her because she was totally uninterested in her surroundings and spent long periods of time sitting quietly by herself. She refused to write anything, claiming she wasn't sure what she might write would be her original idea. She lost all confidence in herself. I felt guilty and responsible for her sadness.

While we were recovering from our ordeal, the newspapers in Boston reported that Helen had collapsed and was feared to have had a mental breakdown. Most of Helen's problems were blamed on me. And I guess rightfully so. I began to doubt myself. I had made many enemies in Boston and should never have allowed *The Frost King* to be published. When Helen succumbed to melancholy, refused to talk, and sat in silence, I escaped my guilt and fear by saddling a horse and recklessly galloping through the countryside to clear my head. Oh, how therapeutic the fresh out-of-doors! I think I may have gone mad without those little outings.

Dr. Bell and his assistant, Mr. Hitz, conducted an independent investigation of the book affair to clarify what actually had taken place. Both of them were convinced the entire affair was an innocent mistake. Mrs. Canby's book and Helen's book were printed side by side to show the similarities and the differences. Mrs. Canby included a poem she wrote praising Helen and her accomplishments. She wrote me a letter asking me to tell Helen how much she loved her and encouraged her to keep writing. To dispel rumors of her breakdown, new photographs were taken showing a lovely and healthy Helen.

We decided it would be best for Helen to stay home and study in Tuscumbia for the next year. It would be better to stay away from Boston for to protect Helen from dreary publicity. In addition, we had no money for personal expenses. I wrote several letters to Mr. Aganos on Helen's behalf, asking him to send us school supplies for the year's study. He would not reply to me, but we finally received a much-needed package. In time, our wounds healed, and we proceeded with our lessons.

*   *   *

Grover Cleveland was running for president again, and Captain Keller was writing every influential person who had supported Helen asking for their assistance obtaining the position of U.S. marshal. Most of them had pledged their support elsewhere, and he did not get the position. Many of our supporters were offended by his boldness.

Captain Keller insisted that Helen and I accompany him to Grover Cleveland's inaugural address, thinking it may help him get the sought-after position. He persuaded Mr. Hitz to invite us to be his guests in Washington. Mr. Hitz had pulled away from me because I thwarted his friendship, which was becoming too personal. He had written me several times, and I had not responded.

I begged Mr. Aganos to meet us there to ease the tension, but he didn't respond to my letters. I was frantically trying to get his support for Helen and me again but had not been successful. All of the letters I wrote him were written with love and kindness, but he wasn't moved and wouldn't respond to me. I heard that he had actually been undermining my accomplishments to the extent that he called Helen "a living lie." Our friendship with him was completely severed.

Our trip to Washington was fruitless. Captain Keller was not even invited to call on the Clevelands. He begged Dr. Bell and Mr. Hitz to see if they could find him and James jobs in Washington. Of course they never did. I doubt if they even tried.

20

LOOKING FOR SCHOOLS

At Dr. Bell's request, we returned to Boston in May 1893 so Helen could break ground for Dr. Bell's new Volta building where research was to be done to benefit the deaf. Mr. Hitz proudly stood beside Helen as the new superintendent of Volta. I believe Dr. Bell thought this trip would also alleviate our fears of someday returning to Boston.

At Dr. Bell's insistence, we arranged to visit several schools for the deaf. We visited the Northampton Pennsylvania Institution, Rochester School for the Deaf, and the Clark School.

*   *   *

During that summer, Helen and Dr. Bell surprised me with a trip to Niagara Falls. I knew something was afoot because Helen had been excited for several days and couldn't keep from smiling. Dr. Bell arranged for a friend, Edmund Lyon, to escort us. We stayed in a beautiful hotel close to the falls and the following day went exploring. How magnificent! I believe Helen enjoyed it more than anyone. She stood in awe as she felt the powerful vibrations of the tumultuous waterfall. The power and energy of the falls were exhilarating, and I felt my soul was cleansed and all my cares dissolved. We took the elevator a hundred and twenty feet down to see the whirlpools in the gorge. Dr. Bell knew exactly what I needed. This was the most wonderful gift I had ever received.

*   *   *

We lounged luxuriously for the remainder of the summer submerged in the love and care of Mrs. Hopkins. I always looked forward to spending time with her. She was like a mother to me, and Cape Cod was my home base. She and I took Helen on the same adventures we had taken when I was close to Helen's age and attending Perkins.

How we enjoyed our time at the beach watching the light of the long days fade and the sound of the gulls as they searched for a resting spot to spend the night. We had numerous picnics, romped and played with the dog, swam, and just sat on the porch and chatted.

A few friends visited, but thankfully it was usually just the three of us. Helen and Mrs. Hopkins adored each other. Mrs. Hopkins was happiest when she was mothering both of us, making sure we ate well and got plenty of sleep and sunshine. We never talked about Mr. Aganos, who was still her employer.

*   *   *

In the later part of summer, we left Cape Cod to stay with Mr. Wade and his family again, basking in the richness of his Pennsylvania estate. Mrs. Wade and her son Archer invited us to go to the 1893 world's fair in Chicago. We were delighted and accepted their invitation. A change of plans at the last minute and it ended up that Dr. Bell escorted us to the fair. We met him in Washington.

What a thrill for both of us to attend the world fair. We were there three weeks and spent every moment exploring. The organizers of the fair led us around the grounds and permitted Helen to touch everything with her hands. She didn't miss a thing.

*   *   *

After a short time in Tuscumbia, we returned to live on Mr. Wade's estate where Dr. John D. Irons tutored Helen for the school year. He taught her Latin and higher math. Dr. Irons could not fingerspell to Helen, so I interpreted for him. I would have preferred that she be in school with other children, but we did not have the financial resources at that time or a school that I liked.

On my regular long walks out-of-doors in the beautiful countryside, I had time to ponder our next move. Many ideas swarmed through my head as I sat under an especially nice large black oak tree, inhaling the fresh late-summer air. I could smell the scent of the approaching fall. Off in the distance, a train rolled by, and a cow moaned in the pasture. How I loved this tranquil place.

We spent the fall surrounded by colorful trees and a snowy winter with the Wades and returned to Tuscumbia in the spring. We were to stay in Tuscumbia until the following fall when hopefully Mr. Keller would have the funds to send us to school. Helen stayed busy working on projects to raise funds for the local library in Tuscumbia, wrote letters, and read several books. I was glad that we were invited to functions in the area to break the monotony at Ivy Green.

I wrote Dr. Bell many times asking him if there was anything he could do to help us raise funds to hasten our return to school. He suggested I speak at his Association for the Promotion of Speech at Chautauqua during the summer. It may open up some doors and provide funding for us. I was terrified of speaking on my own but felt obligated to say yes to my dear friend. The remainder of spring and early summer I worried over my speech.

*   *   *

The speech was titled "The Instruction of Helen Keller." In it I expressed my feelings that every child is capable of learning if they are taught properly. They have to love learning, and reading was essential. I stressed that children must also spend a great deal of time out-of-doors experiencing and learning about the wonders of nature. It's much better than learning facts about nature in the classroom, and a lot more fun. The strict schedules and rules of many educational institutions attempted to force a child to learn but actually hampered learning. Children must want to learn and love to learn. Learning should be fun.

Helen and I met Dr. Bell in Chautauqua midsummer to attend the conference. There looked to be several hundred people in the audience. After I was introduced, I nervously approached the podium. I had been in front of thousands of people before, speaking for Helen while she fingerspelled in my hand, but speaking on my own terrified me. I froze and could not speak. Embarrassed I quickly left the stage, and Dr. Bell graciously read my speech for me.

Fortunately, no one seemed to mind my unease at the podium, and my speech was very well received.

While there, we met John Wright and Dr. Thomas Humason who were opening a school in New York in the fall to teach language to the deaf. They asked to hear Helen speak and afterward told me they thought they could improve her speech if she attended their school.

21

WRIGHT-HUMASON SCHOOL

With welcome donations from one of our good friends John Spaulding, we entered the Wright-Humason School in New York in October 1894. Helen at the age of fourteen was the only student who was both blind and deaf. Twenty-one students attended the school of which fourteen were girls. I was delighted to have Helen around so many girls her own age. The school was located near Central Park in an area that had a country look and feel to it. We still were able to take long walks in a beautiful setting and rode horses regularly in the park.

We continued studies of arithmetic, English literature, and United States history. Dr. Humason worked regularly with Helen to improve her speech. She was excited and actually had dreams of talking normally and even singing. I hated to see her get her hopes up but refrained from discouraging her speech studies. Perhaps she would be able to speak normally and sing, but I very much doubted it. I held my tongue and was very careful what I said because I didn't want to alienate the teachers there, like I had at Perkins. I didn't like the structure and rules of the school but managed to keep my thoughts to myself.

Because the school was located in the city, the children went on wonderful expeditions to museums, the popular new Statue of Liberty, and various special events. I described everything we saw to Helen. Many of the museums graciously allowed Helen to touch priceless exhibits.

Of course Helen drew lots of attention from the elite of New York City, much to my chagrin. We attended most of the functions we were invited to, and I constantly reminded myself that we were not in a financial position to turn away these generous people. I had to keep myself in check and watch what I said and how I said it.

I don't know why I was so uncomfortable around these people. I guess they were nice enough to me, but I always felt like an outsider. I didn't fit in. I felt lonely while in the midst of the crowds of people surrounding us. It was as though I was merely a fixture, a conduit attached to Helen's hand and speaking to her and for her. I was ignored until someone took notice of my existence next to Helen. Then, I usually received a forced, polite smile and a second or so of small talk.

My feelings and accomplishments went unnoticed. It's not at all that I wanted to take away from Helen. I was delighted that she was radiant with all of the attention. I just would like to have had a little more recognition and would have loved having some of my very own close friends. Oh, if they only had known the story of my life. What a scandal that would cause! But I would never let that happen. Helen didn't even know.

Helen did well at this school. Her speech even improved slightly the first few months, but that was all. Others were beginning to be able to understand her, but her speech never did improve to the point where she was comfortable.

My heart ached, however, that even though she participated in all of the activities of the school, she was different than all of the other children who were just hearing impaired; and special accommodations were always required. The other girls were polite and included Helen when they remembered to, but of course they were busy teenage girls and sometimes forgot that Helen couldn't see them. She beamed whenever they paid any attention to her.

In February I received word that our key financial backer, John Spaulding, had died. He had promised to provide lifelong support for Helen but had failed to put it in writing. His heirs did not want to continue supporting Helen but did give a lump sum of $7,000 to Helen's education fund. This was the loss of a good friend as well as a critical blow to our continuing financial support.

The end of our second and final year at Wright-Humason was approaching quickly, and I had no idea what we would do next. I wrote regularly to Dr. Bell and Mr. Hitz asking for assistance in getting funds for our support and Helen's continuing education. Dr. Bell insisted that a formal trust needed to be established. Also, financial supporters in Boston wanted Helen to go to school in the Boston area.

I think his concern was that Captain Keller would declare himself manager of our funds and spend the money for his family and the upkeep of his small estate. Dr. Bell was having trouble finding someone who would manage a trust fund for us. He was correct in his thinking; however, nothing was happening, and I didn't really want to return to Tuscumbia where the family was struggling.

The final school year soon ended, and we spent most of our summer with Mrs. Hopkins. Three weeks were also spent with our generous friends the Chamberlins at their large house on a lake in Wrentham, located just outside Boston. What a beautiful place. It was peppered with large maple, poplar, ash, and fruit trees that shaded the picnics we had with the families of the area. Many afternoons were spent bobbing around in a small rowboat on the lake with our large straw hats and umbrellas protecting us from the summer sun and trailing our fingers in the cool water.

Helen never tired of exploring the out-of-doors. She felt the passing of flying insects and made a game of detecting the location of flowers from their scent and identifying their color. I think she probably remembered colors from infancy.

*   *   *

Soon after our return to Cape Cod, I received word that Captain Keller had died. When I told Helen her father had died, she suffered intense sorrow. More than I could ever have anticipated.

I had not prepared Helen for death. I had experienced enough of it in my childhood that I wanted to shelter her from it. All communications Helen received were through me. Her emotional reactions were dictated by what I communicated to her. I chose what she was allowed to hear and, ultimately, feel. Over the years I had actually told her when to hug or kiss someone and get hugs and kisses in return.

I had failed to realize that Helen's emotions had developed on their own and were as strong, sensitive, and personal as any seeing and hearing person. I felt terrible.

We immediately made plans to travel to Tuscumbia, but Mrs. Keller telegraphed us telling us not to return. It was the hottest time of the year and the sickliest season in Tuscumbia. She did not want Helen exposed to it.

22

CAMBRIDGE, OCTOBER 1896

Since Helen was a young girl, she had dreamed of attending Radcliffe College. She actually wanted to go to Harvard, but it did not admit women. Helen applied for admittance to Radcliffe; and Arthur Gilman, the director of the school, reluctantly accepted her as a student to Cambridge School for Young Ladies, a school that prepared students for admission to Radcliffe. Fortunately, we had successfully acquired funds from our friends to move to Cambridge.

I hated being back in a structured school environment again, but Helen was very happy there and delved into her studies with relish. I interpreted every class for her, and we diligently studied every evening. I was not allowed to sit with her and interpret for exams because Mr. Gilman was suspicious that I was giving her answers. Mr. Gilman himself acted as interpreter. Helen was uncomfortable taking exams without me. However, at the end of the first year, she passed all of her exams with flying colors. In English and German, she received honors. Mr. Gilman was astonished at Helen's ability to learn so quickly and retain information. Helen was delighted when her sister Mildred joined us six months after the semester started.

The original plan was to have Helen attend Cambridge for five years, but after her first year, Mr. Gilman and I decided she could finish the courses there in three years. Shortly thereafter, I decided to push Helen a little bit harder so that we could get through Cambridge sooner and complete our studies in two instead of three years. I was afraid our supporters might not want to support three years at Cambridge. We needed them for Radcliffe College. Mr. Gilman disagreed with me, and I sternly reminded him that I was the one who made the decisions for Helen. The timing for this incident was terrible.

Our second year at Cambridge began well enough, but soon Helen's work deteriorated. This year was devoted primarily to math, which was a subject Helen hated and struggled with. She had never liked or done well with math. In addition, the books in Braille were delayed, and I had to read and interpret all of her math problems. It was difficult for us both.

At the age of seventeen, Helen had problems with her menstrual periods and had to spend a few days each month in bed. With her grades suffering and absences from class, Mr. Gilman's immediate reaction was that I was overworking Helen, and he wrote as much to her mother. Dr. Bell, Mrs. Keller, and Mrs. Hopkins were just a few of the people who got involved; and they determined I was pushing Helen too hard. From what they were told, the consensus was that Helen and I should be separated and Mr. Gilman authorized as Helen's guardian. Gilman was delighted to take charge and credit for Helen's achievements at Cambridge.

When he called me into his office and told me he was taking over responsibility of Helen, I was furious. I demanded that I be returned to the position of Helen's companion and teacher or I would leave the school with both Helen and Mildred. He informed me that it was a "done deal" and that I was no longer needed. I was asked to leave.

No words can describe my feelings that horrible day. My world came to an end. I had suddenly lost part of myself. Helen and I had been as one for nearly nine years. I had nothing else and could not bear to live without her by my side. I seriously contemplated suicide. Then, something deep inside reminded me that Helen needed me as much as I needed her. I could not let her down and had to fight for her.

I went to the home of some friends in Boston and the next morning returned to Cambridge and demanded to see Helen and Mildred. I refused to leave until I saw them. Afraid of a dreadful scene, Helen and Mildred were finally brought to me. I told them what had happened, and Helen and I tearfully clung to each other until she was pulled from me and taken away.

Mildred got word to me a few days later that Helen wouldn't eat or sleep and acted like she was having a nervous breakdown. They were leaving to return to the home of the Chamberlins in Wrentham. I immediately sent Mrs. Keller, Dr. Bell, and Mrs. Hutton, our key fund-raiser, telegrams telling them we urgently needed them.

Mrs. Keller and Dr. Bell's assistant, Mr. Hitz, arrived a few days later and learned what had taken place. After seeing Helen and the state she was in and hearing Mildred's account of the events that took place, Mrs. Keller had a change of heart and put me back in charge of Helen. We dropped out of Cambridge and stayed at Wrentham with the Chamberlins, hired a private tutor, and continued our preparation for Radcliffe. Of course Mr. Gilman was furious.

I was deeply depressed and exhausted when we settled down on the Chamberlins' farm. I didn't feel like doing anything and spent most the time I wasn't in class spelling to Helen wandering the grounds or sitting in my room. I was so tired of fighting and wasn't certain I could continue on. I'm afraid I wasn't very good company for my dear Helen. She was concerned about me and sat many hours by my side quietly holding my hand.

During the darkness of my depression, I wondered how it came to be that an uneducated, homeless person such as myself was given the responsibility I now had. What qualifications did I have? None. I had made many enemies and felt guilty that I had pushed my dear Helen so hard at times. Who else did I have in my life that I cared for, and who cared for me? Without Helen, I was nothing.

I pondered the events of my life and felt self-pity. Then feeling the warmth of Helen's hand in mine, I remembered the child at my side. This blind/deaf child was connected to the world through me. Only me. I couldn't possibly let her down. She was my joy, my heart, my life. Soon I was myself again, determined to give this child a chance to accomplish her every goal and desire. I lived for Helen. That's why I was here.

*   *   *

After three years and a lot of hard work, we achieved our goal! We were accepted at Radcliffe College and started school the fall of 1890. Helen was twenty years old, and I was thirty-four. Our last few years had not been easy. Helen had a goal, and I pushed both of us as hard as I could to help her achieve that goal. I know I was very demanding and probably unreasonable at times. I had to remind myself regularly that she was more important than the goal and let her rest from the rigors of study.

I needed the rest as well. My eyes bothered me, and I was exhausted from the hours and hours of fingerspelling to Helen. I didn't let Helen know how tired I was, and we prepared eagerly for Radcliffe.

We heard nothing from Mr. Gilman, the founder of both Radcliffe and Cambridge colleges.

23

RADCLIFFE, 1900

Radcliffe College was founded in 1879 as a school for women since women were not allowed to attend Harvard. We were entering Mr. Gilman's territory again, and I was very uncomfortable. My bouts of melancholy and depression had increased since our problems at Cambridge. I hated what people had taken Helen and me through just prior to our departure from that despicable school. I had to keep a wary eye out for interference while we were at Radcliffe. Oh, how at times I hated people! Sometimes I'm not certain whether I pushed Helen to succeed for herself or to show people what I could do.

We rented a small house on the outskirts of Cambridge near the Charles River. I was glad to get away from the hustle and bustle of school every afternoon and return to our little house surrounded by trees and fields where I could breathe. We had a housekeeper named Bridget. The house had two tiny bedrooms, a parlor, study, and dining room. I hung lace curtains in the parlor, and over time we accumulated all the furnishings we needed. We were very comfortable in our little home. Helen was the only student living off campus. It would have been nice for Helen to live on campus with her friends, but I could not have borne it.

The next four years were difficult for both of us. We had very few books in Braille. Four to five hours of class time were spent rapidly spelling lectures into Helen's hand. We always hurried back to our home so Helen could record what we remembered of the lecture on her Braille typewriter. It was impossible to take notes during class because our hands were busy with fingerspelling the lecture. At times it was difficult for Helen to keep up. She grew despondent and worked herself (and me) even harder. Before long Helen could read my finger signing and at the same time follow along with a Braille book. She could read my hand as quickly as the hearing could hear.

To my dismay, two proctors were assigned to work with Helen when she took exams. The administration didn't trust us. Dean Irwin wanted to dispel any question that Helen was the student and not me. I actually had to leave the building. I certainly would have preferred to be Helen's interpreter, but I did not argue. It was slower for Helen because their fingerspelling was slower and sometimes a little different, but she managed to do well on all of her tests.

One of the proctors had a handsome son Helen's age who became interested in her. She had become quite a beautiful, intelligent young lady and was always pleasant and eager to meet new people. Mrs. Keller had a fit when she heard about it and demanded that the young man be kept away from Helen. I agreed at the time but have wondered on many occasions if that was fair to Helen. She had no opportunity to love a man other than through platonic relationships.

Once Helen's fellow classmates got to know Helen and felt at ease with her, she had many friends. It took time for them to feel comfortable directing all of their conversations to Helen through me. I was much older than they were and didn't have anything in common with them. I was simply the means through which they communicated with Helen.

We attended most of the class functions. The students loved Helen and pooled their money to buy Helen a little Boston terrier that she named Phiz. Helen joined her classmates in the swimming pool and loved riding around town on the back of a tandem bicycle with the girls. I was by her side in the pool to interpret instructions and conversations and in the front seat of the tandem bicycle. I certainly got good exercise participating with Helen in all of the events. In December of her first year at Radcliffe, her class elected her vice president.

It was a lonely life for me. The faculty only talked to me when necessary. The teachers never went out of their way to provide any extra assistance to us or even talk to me about Helen's progress. It was obvious Mr. Gilman had a hand in their behavior. I was so tired at the end of the day I wasn't able to write regular letters to our friends and supporters. Letters were always welcome at our home and reminded me that there was life outside of Radcliffe and people who cared for me. I missed my long chats with Dr. Bell.

From the strain of four to five hours fingerspelling to Helen in class and evening studies, my sight began failing quickly. I was only able to read a printed page if I had my nose nearly touching the paper. My eyes were sore and red again. I didn't tell Helen. But she soon figured out that I couldn't read any notes I had taken. She insisted I have my eyes checked, and fortunately the ophthalmologist said I just needed to give my eyes a good rest. But he insisted that if I didn't rest them, I would go blind. I was so fearful of going blind again that I followed all of his instructions and did not overtax my eyes. Helen told me after she graduated that she was so concerned for my welfare that she didn't admit to needing my help with her studies.

*   *   *

Year two at Radcliffe was easier on both of us. There were more literature courses on Helen's agenda, and with the encouragement of Professor Charles Copeland, she began to write. Soon, her articles were published in the *Ladies' Home Journal*, and we began earning some of our own income. Three thousand dollars were offered Helen to write and publish the story of her life. We needed the money badly and accepted the offer, but I was soon concerned at the pressure this was putting on Helen and the effect it had on her schoolwork. I couldn't give her the help she needed because I had to rest my eyes and hands.

By 1904 Helen and I had met three presidents of the United States, Presidents Grover Cleveland, William McKinley, and Theodore Roosevelt. The name Helen Keller was known throughout the world. Our every move was publicized.

*   *   *

I told one of our friends, Lenore Smith, about my concern for Helen's ability to write a book at the same time she was attending classes. Lenore introduced us to a twenty-five-year-old man by the name of John Macy who was an instructor of English at Harvard.

He was a tall, thin young man with a pleasant face and dark hair and wore wire-rimmed glasses. John was born into a middle-class family in Detroit, Michigan. He had attended Harvard on a scholarship. He was extremely popular in college with both teachers and students and while there achieved an outstanding academic record. He was known as a renegade and was very outspoken about his beliefs. I believe that's one of the things I admired about him most.

John was willing and eager to help Helen edit the book. What a godsend! John spent many hours at our home with Helen and me. He was very impressed with Helen's literary capabilities and her incredible memory. He very quickly learned to fingerspell with her.

I loved it when he visited. The three of us laughed and talked and took long walks in the woods by the river. He enjoyed our company as much as we enjoyed his, and soon he was at our home most of the time. He worked around the house and yard and strung a rope between trees so Helen could walk alone following the rope. She was delighted to have independent time out-of-doors. He built bookcases, stools, and a table and made numerous needed repairs.

John always raved about my abilities as a teacher and wanted to write articles about me. I was pleased and welcomed his kind words but adamantly refused and made him promise to keep me out of the papers. He told me many times that what I had done was as impressive and important as what Helen had accomplished. His compliments were very much appreciated, and I could tell they were heartfelt. However, I did not want my story told. Since he was around the house so much, I was afraid he would find and read my diaries; and while he and Helen were busy, one day I burned them.

Over the next three years, John and I became lovers. It was wonderful to be held and loved. I was eleven years older than John, but it did not affect our relationship. We were passionately in love. He was only three years older than Helen! I felt young and pretty when I was with John. I was sincerely happy, and my bouts of depression evaporated into the essence of his love.

John became Helen's literary agent, and her book *The Story of My Life* was published in her junior year at Radcliffe in 1903. It was dedicated to our dear friend and supporter Dr. Alexander Graham Bell. It became very popular and the subject of many newspaper editorials, and it provided us with much-needed funds.

*   *   *

Helen graduated from Radcliffe College with a bachelor of arts degree cum laude on June 28, 1904. Graduation ceremonies were held at the Sanders Theater auditorium in Cambridge. There were ninety-five students in her graduating class. How proud I was when we mounted the steps to receive the diploma. I knew in my heart that I had graduated also. How I wish I could have received my own diploma. Most of our friends attended the ceremony. Unfortunately, Mrs. Keller could not attend due to illness. Helen was very disappointed.

24

WRENTHAM, 1905-1913

With shares of our benefactor John Spaulding's sugar stock, we purchased a beautiful old home in Wrentham, Massachusetts. Tall granite posts stood at attention and welcomed us as we entered the drive. The house was large; and the land surrounding it was peppered with pines, spruces, poplar, and several varieties of fruit trees. Privet hedges and flowers bordered the drive. Berry bushes behind the house were higher than my head.

Grape vines heavy with grapes wove around a trellis in the backyard. The thick aroma of the grapes surrounded us when we sat on the bench beneath the trellis. If the breeze blew just in the right direction, I could smell the grapes while I worked in the kitchen. Nothing tastes as good as a juicy ripe grape picked right off the vine.

The farm needed a great deal of attention. The barn door was coming off the hinges, the porch steps needed repair, and there was a lot of cleaning to be done. I looked forward to the work. However, we were exhausted from our strenuous senior year studies and always being surrounded by throngs of people, so we put off starting our refurbishing and rested.

I was not feeling well. I was certain it was just the strain of the last few years at Radcliffe. My bones hurt, my eyes were sore, stomach problems plagued me, and I was nervous and irritable. Sometimes I grew very melancholy. The work on our home would have to wait while I recovered.

As I look back, I believe what bothered me most and contributed to my health and emotional problems was that Helen was now an adult, and the future was unclear. Would we still have enough financial contributions for our support? Could we support ourselves through Helen's writing and perhaps lecturing? I didn't think I could possibly take the strain and tension of travel and lecturing. At thirty-eight I felt old, tired, and afraid.

Helen also needed rest after years of vigorous study and the whirlwind activities of graduation. We did nothing but lie around, take naps, and stroll the grounds of our property for several days. We especially enjoyed long horseback rides. How I loved my horses. The fresh country air and rest soon invigorated both of us. Helen began writing, and I was up and about busying myself on our farm. John Macy was there as often as possible to help us. He loved the farm as much as we did.

Soon the house was cozy with lace curtains and table covers, shiny clean floors, fresh painted walls, and vases of multicolored flowers everywhere. The sparkling clean windows were open to let in the fresh summer breeze. It was so wonderfully quiet. Many times I stopped what I was doing and just listened to the quiet. Then I would hear a birdcall, or a fly buzz by. All of the sounds were earth sounds.

When the house was finally in order, I set about to conquer the yard and garden. When John was there, we companionably worked side by side pulling weeds, trimming rosebushes, and planting flowers and even a late garden. He was wonderful company as well as a talented handyman. He fixed the barn door and replaced the porch steps for us.

The rich smell and feel of the dirt, the sun on my back, and the fresh air in my lungs healed me and made me feel young again. Chickadees sang to me while I toiled. Ladybugs enjoyed resting on my arms, and I could hear but not see little flying insects circling around me and inspecting my work. Several times a day I forced Helen from her writing to help me so she could experience the joy of the earth as I did. I fingerspelled everything I saw and heard. She couldn't hear or see, but her sense of feel was so sensitive and her imagination so astute that she could feel what I described. I honestly believe that we could transmit feelings and pictures between us: we were so close.

After supper we sat on the front porch in the swing or in the rocking chairs drinking iced tea and discussing our accomplishments of the day. Helen was writing articles for several magazines to supplement our income and eager to share what she had written. After we retreated to the house to escape the mosquitoes, we played chess or checkers, read Helen's work, or just talked. We were very content.

John's visits always livened up our days and evenings. John's stories and antics filled our home with laughter. Sometimes he coaxed us from our chores, and we packed a picnic lunch and headed to one of the nearby lakes. If we were lucky, he fished and caught pickerel or trout for our dinner.

John was becoming a permanent fixture at our home. He lacked funds and soon gave up his room in town and moved in with us. When he had business in Boston, he stayed with a friend. I loved this intelligent, energetic young man and wasn't certain he should be living with us. He started hinting of marriage. We had a lot of interests in common, including Helen, and never tired of being in each other's company. But I was eleven years older than him. I wasn't sure I wanted to or knew how to be a wife. Could I be devoted to two people?

By the end of the year, John was begging me to marry him. I vacillated back and forth as to whether to, and finally, I agreed. We married the following spring with the understanding of course that Helen would continue to live with us.

The wedding took place on May 2, 1905, in the early afternoon in the living room of our home in Wrentham. I was thirty-nine and John was twenty-eight. About twenty guests attended the ceremony. Our own beautiful early spring flowers adorned every surface of the house. I wore a new dark blue dress with white silk at the waist. My normally unruly hair was pulled back from my face, and curls fashionably covered the back of my head. John wore a gray frock coat and looked as handsome as ever. Helen was in the wedding party of course and wore a beautiful moss green dress. She looked stunning. Lenore, the friend who had introduced us to John, fingerspelled the service to Helen.

The wedding vows were followed by a small luncheon. I had baked our wedding cake myself. By late afternoon John and I were on our way to Boston to board a boat for a New Orleans honeymoon. Helen went to Tuscumbia with her mother.

We were only gone a few days, and I missed Helen terribly. Her mother still didn't fingerspell well, and I knew Helen was lonesome and bored. John suggested we go to Tuscumbia, pick up Helen, and go back to Wrentham. I believe he missed her as much as I did. When we arrived at Ivy Green, Helen was delighted to see us.

*   *   *

The three of us fell into a comfortable routine on our farm in Wrentham. Our garden thrived with all of the attention, and I was able to can lots of fresh vegetables for our winter meals. John traveled back and forth from the city giving lectures whenever possible but spent most of his time at home working with Helen editing her books and articles. Articles he wrote about Helen were published all over the world. People never lost interest hearing about Helen.

John lovingly strung ropes between trees and out into the meadow so Helen could roam around on her own. I always kept my eyes on her when she went on excursions by herself. Like me, she was attracted to trees, and John made sure her rope paths guided her to her favorite ones. She stood in the shade of the trees and touched their trunks as though communicating with them. I'm certain she was.

We took long walks through wooded trails that were filled with the sounds of all the little inhabitants living there. The trees were full of birds busily looking for their dinner, calling to their families and chatting with their neighbors. The thick tall shrubs and bushes hugging the trail were alive with activity. John and I were quiet and didn't talk on our walks so Helen could feel only the vibrations of the precious trees, bushes, and creatures surrounding us. I spelled everything I saw and heard into her hand. Quietly spelling for her what I saw and sensed seemed to make everything even more vivid to me. I communicated the beauty I saw and how it felt to me, and she was able to see and feel the life and beauty of it in her own way.

We drove our new car through the picturesque country town of Wrentham, stopping to speak to friends, and cooled ourselves with ice cream from the local ice cream parlor. We had several picnics over the summer in wooded areas or beside a local lake with our close neighbors and friends. Everyone brought a delicious dish to share, and after stuffing ourselves, we rested in the shade of a tree or strolled along the banks of the lake. We were delighted when Mrs. Hopkins, Dr. Bell and his family, or the Wades came to join us.

*   *   *

John and I were very passionate; however, to my extreme disappointment, I didn't conceive. I wanted a child of my own so badly. I had female problems and probably was too old to conceive. I put it out of my head and determined to enjoy our lives without a child of our own. Our happy threesome enjoyed each other's company; and we had two loving dogs, Phiz and Kaiser, as well as horses, chickens, and one old bossy rooster. Friends visited, we traveled a little, and Helen accepted invitations to speak at various local events. She and John continued publishing articles. During this time, her book *The World I Live In* was published.

John and Helen became Socialists, and both joined the Socialist Party of Massachusetts to protest the government systems and oppose the upcoming war. John introduced her to Karl Marx and subscribed to the German socialist magazine written in Braille. Helen spoke and wrote several articles opposing World War I and became deeply involved in the women's suffrage movement.

I didn't agree with many of John and Helen's philosophies and didn't participate in the Socialist activities with them. The Socialists were too revolutionary and militant for me. I had fought all of my life. My fighting days, I hoped, were over.

I was just happy that Helen's main focus remained on improving conditions for the blind. She served on the Massachusetts Commission for the Blind and wrote numerous articles for the prevention of blindness. One of her accomplishments was to persuade hospitals around the nation to prevent infant blindness by putting a drop of nitrate of silver into each eye soon after birth.

The three of us visited the 1905 Louisiana Purchase Exposition in St. Louis where October 18 was declared Helen Keller Day. The hall was filled to capacity to see Helen, and so many people surrounded us after her talk that I feared for our safety. We realized we had to be more cautious when we made public appearances.

Since Helen was in the eyes of the public a great deal, we arranged for her to have eye surgery to remove her eyes and replace them with glass eyes. Her left eye had always protruded, which is why her photographs were always taken of the right side of her face. Helen began taking voice lessons again from Charles White, a singing instructor at the Boston Conservatory of Music who told us he was certain he could improve her speech. He had invented a special program for the deaf, dumb, and blind to increase the flexibility of their vocal cords.

*   *   *

I received word in the fall of 1906 that Mr. Aganos had died while living in Greece. I have always regretted that our friendship had ended after *The Frost King* affair. He had been so good to me while I attended Perkins and was responsible for my position to teach Helen. How I'd love to have been able to tell him how much I loved him and appreciated his help before he died. However, even at his memorial service that I thankfully did not attend, I was criticized.

During this four-year period, we also lost dear friends Samuel Clemens and Edward Hale. How empty we felt after our good friends left our world.

*   *   *

Tenseness developed between John and me, and we started to quarrel a great deal. He complained constantly about the amount of time I devoted to Helen. I don't think he realized before we were married just how much

Helen depended on me. When he wasn't working with her or she wasn't busy reading or writing, I was her only contact with the outside world. I led her through daily activities and, when she wasn't working, was by her side talking to her. That was not going to change.

However, I have often wondered if Helen was the problem or if it was really the result of the age difference between us. I had gained a great deal of weight over the last year, and my health was not very good. I didn't have the vitality that I had when he met me. He loved Helen, and I believe she was just his excuse for our deteriorating relationship.

John took a position in Schenectady, New York, to work as secretary for the Socialist administration and hoped to find a position for Helen and have us move there with him. The separation was good for all of us. However, Helen and I never did move to Schenectady.

We were very short on funds and began writing letters to various organizations in hopes of obtaining speaking engagements. We had maintained our relationships with our old friends and wrote them, asking for advice and assistance. Helen finally accepted a pension from Carnegie. For some time she had refused to apply for the pension which provides funds to people needing assistance whose activities have made major contributions to society.

Around that same time, I began experiencing a great deal of pain in my stomach, and my menstrual periods were heavy. I lost so much blood each month that I was weak most of the time. I finally went to see a doctor; and I was rushed to St. Vincent's Hospital in Brookline, Massachusetts, where they immediately performed a hysterectomy. I was anemic, and the surgery nearly killed me. After the surgery, I was so near death that I couldn't even fingerspell to Helen when she visited.

When John heard I had been hospitalized, he took a leave of absence from his job and stayed by my side. His constant presence and the visits from Helen gave me reason to live, and I slowly recovered. Helen went to Washington to stay with our friend Lenore Smith while I completed my recovery. When I was finally released from the hospital and returned to Wrentham, Helen and Mrs. Keller helped John take care of me.

25

LECTURE CIRCUIT

About four months after I was released from the hospital, Helen was scheduled to give her first speech in Montclair, New Jersey, using her own voice. Unfortunately, stage fright overpowered her, and she left the stage in tears. I finished her speech for her. After the program, we were deluged with people congratulating Helen for a wonderful speech. They scheduled several more engagements, and Helen regained her confidence and was able to speak.

Helen gave a lecture to the Harvard International Otological Congress in August of that year. Her speech had improved to the point where the audience was able to follow some of what she was saying, but I repeated most of the speech after she had finished. Whenever she spoke, I watched the audience closely to see if they understood what she said. If I thought they had not, I repeated her speech to them.

This arrangement worked out very well because people wanted to hear her speak her own words but also wanted to know what she was saying. Helen was always disappointed that she didn't speak quite clearly enough, but she certainly kept trying.

In May 1913, Helen and I were well into the year's scheduled lectures around the country when John left for holiday in Europe for five months. Our relationship was not good, and I was happy to have him out of our lives for a while. I had to concentrate on keeping up with Helen on our strenuous lecture circuit and couldn't worry over John.

We spent the remainder of the summer in the Alleghenies near Pittsburg at the home of a wealthy friend and supporter Mrs. William Thaw. We bathed in the luxury of a full staff that prepared all of our meals and maintained the house. Mrs. Thaw had business to attend to and only joined us for a few days. We took long walks breathing in the wonderful woody air. It was a time of complete relaxation for us.

* * *

When John returned, he rented an apartment in Boston. We stayed with him between lectures, but I was very uncomfortable around him. He was drinking a great deal and looked at my obesity with disgust. After one particularly violent quarrel, Helen and I left the apartment, and soon after John filed for divorce. However, in spite of threat of divorce, John returned to Wrentham to live with us and then went to our Boston apartment while we traveled throughout Canada to lecture. He had no money to live on his own. I think he spent most of his income on alcohol.

From the letters he wrote Helen while we were traveling, it was apparent that he was drinking heavily. He did not write to me. He ranted and raved about my treatment of him and Helen to Mrs. Keller and accused me of all sorts of abuse. I was accused of being a fraud, and he tried to convince Helen to leave me and let him take care of her business.

Unfortunately Helen and I had a lot of our belongings in the apartment we shared with John in Boston. Some of the things were quite valuable including several articles Helen was in the process of writing. In a drunken stupor, John dropped a cigarette, and the apartment was gutted by fire. He claimed it was an accident, but I was never sure it was.

He sobered up and told me how much he loved me. He begged me to let him move back with us. I relented, and he returned to live with us for a short while in 1916. I know it was foolish, but I wanted him to love me so badly. Shortly after his return, I was ill again. Perhaps that is one reason he started to drink again. I was heavy and sickly and now possibly had a contagious disease. I realized he was actually repulsed by me, and he really didn't love me but needed me. Another argument and he left, and we never lived together again.

I was devastated that our marriage hadn't worked out. I really loved John and yearned for his love and devotion in return. For several months I mourned the loss of my husband and spent most of my time in my bedroom weeping. I had experienced so much loss in my life. When this loss was stacked on top of the rest that had silently lingered in my memory for so many years, the weight became too heavy. I experienced again the pain of all of the losses in my life. I felt unwanted and unloved by everyone except Helen.

Throughout my lifetime, except for the few happy years with my mother that I barely remember, I have been of no consequence to anyone but Helen. For a few years John made me feel loved and needed; and now I had to face the facts that it was not true, sincere, unconditional love. I felt foolish that I had believed he had loved me. I had been used. I should never have trusted my heart to him. Helen was my only reason to live.

Helen and I continued to help him financially for four more years, but it was the end of our marriage. John filed for divorce again after we quit sending him money in 1920, but I never granted him one. I still foolishly hoped that he would quit drinking and come back to me, but that never happened. So I made him suffer and refused to give him a divorce, even when his mother came and begged me to sign the papers. He was forced to live with his deaf-mute girlfriend and never marry.

*   *   *

I was very frail, and the responsibility of Helen and the work required for our lecture tours was too much for me. My weight made it difficult to get around, and I couldn't possibly exercise. My eyes bothered me, and I could no longer see clearly. We were scheduled to go on an extended lecture tour in 1915, and I worried whether I could physically and emotionally do it. We decided we needed an assistant and hired a Scotswoman by the name of Polly Thompson. She was a healthy, energetic, good-looking young woman who immediately relieved me of many tasks. She even learned how to do our hair and nails for public appearances. I was so grateful to have her join us.

One highlight of the 1915 lecture tour for me was the Teacher's Medal I received at the San Francisco fair. I was so pleased to be recognized for my work with Helen, and better yet, the educators in the audience applauded my teaching methods. I was even told I inspired them! They asked me to speak, and I remember pouring my heart out to the audience. I was able to once again express my deep-felt feelings that every child was capable of learning and achieving their goals. But to be successful, we must deinstitutionalize our schools and teach the children to enjoy learning and not be forced to learn. A lot of people approached me after the award and asked numerous questions regarding Helen and how I taught her. They commented that I had broken new ground and were amazed that I achieved Helen's education with little experience of my own and no assistance. They did not look down their noses at me. They actually seemed to look up to me. This was a rare experience, and I basked in the warmth of their compliments and appreciation. Helen was delighted at the attention I was given.

At the age of thirty-six, Helen had become a very popular speaker and in demand all over the country. She was not only recognized for her accomplishments as a blind/deaf woman but also for her opinions. She was well versed about important current affairs. She was asked to speak about the potential of war and attended meetings of the Industrial Workers of the World and the National Woman's Party. She spoke often about the country's labor disputes, race riots, and the farmers' uprising against the draft. I attended all of the meetings to be Helen's eyes and ears.

*   *   *

Polly's mother took ill, and she returned to Scotland. In her absence, we hired another assistant by the name of Peter Fagan suggested to us by John. Peter was twenty-nine years old and had worked for John. John thought very highly of him.

By the time we returned to Wrentham to catch our breath before our next lecture circuit, I had become quite ill. The last few years of travel had taken their toll on me. By April 1916, Helen and I had given over one hundred lectures. I was by her side throughout, fingerspelling and, when necessary, speaking for her. I was totally exhausted. My lungs were congested, and I coughed continuously. I was still deeply depressed over my failed marriage and ashamed of my obesity. I wore only baggy black dresses to cover and hide my ugly body. I was a mess!

The doctor insisted I move to the mountains for a few months, thinking the fresh air might relieve the lung congestion. He told me tests indicated I had the dreaded tuberculosis. Polly had recently returned from Scotland after the death of her mother and accompanied me to Lake Placid, New York, for the winter. Helen returned to Tuscumbia with her mother and Mr. Fagan. Fortunately Mr. Fagan had learned fingerspelling and could communicate with Helen directly. However, in the end it was most unfortunate.

While I was in Lake Placid, Mr. Fagan wooed Helen with his kindness and before the winter was over had convinced her to secretly marry him. I hadn't been around him long enough to really get to know him, but Mrs. Keller was very suspicious of his motives and also was adamant that Helen never marry. She never changed her position that Helen was an invalid and invalids shouldn't marry. When she heard that they had taken out a marriage license, she threw him out of the house.

Apparently he and Helen had a secret meeting and made plans to elope. Mr. Fagan had worked out a complicated scheme to kidnap Helen and take her to Florida to marry. Mrs. Keller somehow heard about it and thwarted the scheme by hurriedly traveling with Helen to Montgomery to her younger daughter Mildred's home. Fagan had not given up, however, and showed up at Mildred's home to get Helen. Mildred's husband met him brandishing a gun. He snuck back one more time in the middle of the night, but fortunately Mildred's husband heard him, and Mr. Fagan left and never returned. Was he truly in love with Helen and willing to be her constant companion, or was he trying to marry her for fame and financial reasons? I never knew for sure.

*   *   *

While all of this was taking place, Polly and I were basking in the sun in Puerto Rico. I had hated Lake Placid and wanted to rest in a sunny, warm place. Everyone discouraged this move, including the doctor. But something told me this was what I should be doing.

We didn't stay in a hotel but instead rented a clean little shack in the hills surrounded by fruit trees, large round ceiba trees that were over seven hundred inches in circumference, tall casuarina, fig trees, and hundreds of colorful parrots, cuckoo, and little tody birds. Oxen grazed the land, and while I enjoyed the fresh bananas, they enjoyed munching on the banana leaves. The temperature reached the high eighties during the day, and the humidity was high.

Evenings were very pleasant. From our little porch, we said good night to the sun and watched it slowly sink into the horizon after brilliant displays of color. Soon after the sunset, millions of stars appeared in the night sky. I had never seen so many stars at one time. Staring into their depth, I felt a oneness with the universe. I felt all weight leave my body and a lightness so light I felt as though I could float into its depth. My worries vanished as I let myself be pulled into the deepness and quiet of forever.

We never lit our lamp at night so we could enjoy the light of the moon and the stars. Also, we had to avoid attracting all of the little flying creatures. We went to bed early to avoid those nuisances. After a few weeks in the sun and on the beach, I felt wonderful. My cough began clearing, and I started feeling energy return to my poor weak body. My depression and melancholy melted into the warm sand and was absorbed deeply into the darkness of the earth. I experienced the feeling of exhilaration for the first time in years.

I wrote regular letters in Braille to my dear Helen. How I would have loved having her there with us. Her letters to me revealed the drama of love that was taking place in her life. I wished I could be there to help her heal her broken heart. In addition to her love affair with Mr. Fagan, she felt out of place with her family. They didn't appreciate her radical views and strong will. She was lonely.

I was angry with her family for not being proud of her ability to have her own opinions and communicate her views. She was showing independence. A totally deaf and blind woman was able to understand all of the serious issues taking place across our country and the world, and her opinion regarding these issues was sought after by millions of people. How could they not marvel at this! My feelings toward the country's problems were not always the same as Helen's, but I would never have squelched her enthusiasm and very seldom discouraged her from sharing her opinions. It made me realize that her family could not take my place. I had to get well and return to her as quickly as possible.

*   *   *

April 6, 1917, I had no choice but return to the United States. War had been declared on Germany. With great reluctance, Polly and I packed and returned to Wrentham. Helen and I were very happy to see each other after a five-month separation and spent hours talking about the events that took place in our lives while we were separated. Being without Helen was like being without part of myself. I believe she felt the same. We were whole again.

Our funds were depleting rapidly, and we were forced to sell our beloved farm in Wrentham. Oh, how I hated to sell that wonderful place where Helen, John, and I had spent so many wonderful years. Helen declared they were the happiest thirteen years of her life. Before moving to a rented cottage in Vermont, I returned to the doctor in Lake Placid for a checkup. After examining me and reviewing my records, the doctor declared me sound and said there had been a paperwork error and I never had tuberculosis. My records and another patient's records had been mixed up.

If I didn't have tuberculosis, then what was wrong with me? At the age of fifty, I felt very ill and was depressed, obese, unable to walk without assistance; and my eyesight was so bad I could hardly read. The doctors could find nothing wrong with me.

After we settled into our rented cottage in Vermont, I concentrated on rest and recovery while Polly and Helen explored the area, taking long hikes and even climbing Whiteface Mountain. I was glad Helen was so comfortable with Polly and enjoyed her company. How I wished I had their energy and zest for life!

When summer came to an end, I was feeling somewhat better, and we decided to look for a small home in New York. We found the perfect place in Forest Hills. It's just what I wanted. A beautiful little Tudor home modeled after garden communities in England. It was quaint with little towers that reminded us of a castle. Beautiful large trees and colorful flowers and bushes surrounded the house. We were only fourteen miles from Times Square and were able to travel frequently to the city to enjoy the many stores and restaurants there. My wonderful Great Dane companion Siegland soon joined us, and our little family was complete.

Helen continued writing and speaking as much as possible against the war and other government issues. Her income from her articles and engagements was very important for our support. However, speaking engagements started dwindling toward the end of the year, and we had to begin discussing other means to make an income.

26

HOLLYWOOD AND VAUDEVILLE

1918-1924

After a year of no income except the pension from Carnegie and donations from our friends and philanthropists, we were desperately in need of more income. The lecture circuit had dried up. I felt we could live on our current income, but Helen was adamant that we couldn't. She told me later she was concerned that if I outlived her, I would have no income.

She had been asked on several occasions to go to Hollywood to film the story of her life. She had no choice and accepted the offer. Soon we were off to Hollywood.

Thank goodness for Polly because I was still weak and unable to be on the set with Helen every day. Many times Polly stood beside Helen as I sat on a chair and watched. The doctors still did not know what was wrong with me. I am certain they thought my illness was in my head, and I was beginning to think so myself. If I could only lose some weight and walk well, I was certain I would feel better, but that was not to be.

Our time in Hollywood making the movie *Deliverance* was a nightmare, especially for me. They didn't portray Helen's life at all. They made up things to attract the public. Helen was dressed and makeup applied unnaturally and acted and spoke completely out of character. Thankfully she was allowed to move around, dance, and show how she communicated.

But that was about all that was really Helen. I was forced to play a small part in the film and refused to cover my fat form with anything other than the large black gowns I had been wearing for several years to cover my obesity.

Several movie stars wanted to meet Helen; and we were introduced to Mary Pickford, Douglas Fairbanks, Lillian Gish, and many more. Again, I felt like an outsider. They definitely looked down on me. Of course it was made worse by my appearance. I was very uncomfortable around these beautiful people. Charlie Chaplin, though, seemed to genuinely like me. I believe we understood each other. We both had been raised in poverty and overcome many hurdles in our lives. We never shared those facts, but when I later heard about his childhood, I realized this was the case.

The movie opened in August 1919 and was a failure! We discovered it was being used as a strikebreaker and was released on the same day the actors had gone on strike. All of the other theaters on Broadway were dark.

*   *   *

Lack of income from *Deliverance* was a big disappointment. We had hoped that money earned from the movie would sustain us for several years. In discussing our options, we were reminded that George Lewis, a musician on the movie set, suggested we consider vaudeville. He had given us contact information for Harry and Herman Weber who were the managers who produced and promoted vaudeville attractions. George told us that people were making a great deal of money in vaudeville. We had totally dismissed this idea as ridiculous. However, after we discussed our options, we realized it was the only way for us to make an income and live comfortably. We contacted the Webers.

*   *   *

We performed our first act in February 1920 in Mt. Vernon, New York. We were on stage twice a day for four years moving to a new venue every week. I agreed to wear an evening gown only if it was black and loose fitting. On cue, I struggled out of my chair behind the curtains and gingerly walked into the horrible glare on stage. Most every performance was to a full house.

I gave a little talk about Helen's accomplishments from the time she was a child and her educational achievements. Then Helen was led to me on stage, and we talked and took questions from the audience. This only took about twenty minutes, then the other scheduled acts took over. There were freak acts, magicians, healers, acrobats, every type of oddity the producers could find. Some of our friends were appalled that we shared the stage with unsavory acts and felt we were making spectacles of ourselves.

Helen loved it and thrived. I hated it and endured, but we made a great deal of money. At one time we were the highest-paid performers on vaudeville, making up to two thousand dollars in one week. We became very wealthy the four years we worked vaudeville.

A year after we began our vaudeville tours, we got word that Mrs. Keller had died. Helen made the difficult decision to continue our tour and not return to Tuscumbia for the funeral. She felt very bad about her mother's unexpected death just as she would any good friend's death. Helen and Mrs. Keller had never been close. Mrs. Keller thought of Helen as an invalid and adamantly disagreed with her politics and our decision to join the vaudeville circuit.

Shortly after Mrs. Keller's death while we were performing in Toronto, I came down with a very bad case of the flu. It was a serious disease in 1921, and many people died. Fortunately, Polly was with us and took my place on stage until I recovered. Then, in 1922, I became ill again with bronchitis; and Polly took my place again. I never returned to the stage. At fifty-six years of age, my health was just too fragile. The last two years of vaudeville, Polly went on stage with Helen. I traveled with them when I could, and we spent the time we weren't traveling at our home in Forest Hills.

When vaudeville was finally behind us, we were able to live comfortably in our little New York home. Helen began working with John Macy on the development of the American Foundation for the Blind, wrote articles, made public appearances with Polly, and began writing her fifth book *My Religion* and sixth book *Midstream.*

*   *   *

On August 2, 1922, we suffered a tremendous loss. Our dear, dear friend Dr. Alexander Graham Bell died. This loving, quiet, unassuming grey-bearded man was our closest friend. He was an amazing man and did so much for the world.

His mother had lost her hearing when he was twelve, and he was determined to break through her barrier of soundlessness. They developed a fingerspelling method to communicate. He then discovered that if he talked into the bone on her forehead, she could hear him and distinguish some words. His research ultimately led to his development of the telegraph, the phonoautograph, and the telephone, from which he became famous. But his proudest achievements were those contributing to the education of the deaf and the establishment of the Volta Laboratory and Bureau to research and educate the deaf.

He was my mentor and my best friend. I was too ill to attend my good friend's funeral.

27

IRELAND, SCOTLAND, AND BRITTANY

At the age of sixty-three, my eyesight, especially my right eye, had deteriorated a great deal. Bright light caused excruciating pain, and I could only read if I wore thick, heavy glasses. I had a cataract, and it became so painful that my right eye was removed. A cataract in my left eye blurred my vision, and I used eyedrops to enlarge the pupils so I could read with the aid of my heavy, thick glasses. I was going blind. A condition I had feared since the time I had lived in darkness as a child.

Against doctors' orders, I frantically read everything I could before the dreaded darkness overtook me. I attended very few of Helen's functions, leaving that to Polly. I enjoyed my time alone with my dogs, especially my beloved Siegland, who had become as old and frail as I. Siegland died that year-1929. It was like losing a child. He had hardly left my side for months. He seemed to understand me, and when I felt especially blue, he put his head in my lap and looked at me with complete love and devotion. Many times a day for weeks after he died, I found myself reaching down by my chair to stroke his head and ears and found only emptiness.

*   *   *

In April 1930, Helen and Polly insisted I accompany them on a speaking circuit of Ireland, England, and Scotland. I had been stubbornly refusing to go, but I realized I was being very selfish. Helen was still young and anxious to travel and wouldn't go without me. While Helen and Polly enjoyed the sea air on deck, I stayed in the cabin. I was not at all anxious to visit my parents' homeland, Ireland. But I had to show enthusiasm for Helen's sake.

I actually ended up enjoying our trip. We timed it well. In Ireland the rhododendrons were at their best, covering the land with color that was accentuated by the blueness of the sky. The air was fresh and clean. It was nice to spend time enjoying the wonders of nature again after hiding myself for months in my room. The weather was perfect.

We celebrated Helen's fiftieth birthday in Ireland basking in the sun at Bray Head in the Wicklow Mountains. Helen was full of energy and enjoyed every moment of our trip. Her face radiated good health.

How I wish I had the energy and vitality to walk amongst the flowers and through the beautiful deep green valleys with Helen and Polly. I would have loved to see and touch all thirty-seven shades of green for which Ireland was known.

Helen insisted that I attempt to find my relatives. I found out that most of them were working-class people. Dad came from a typical large Irish family. They were superstitious, proud, and very happy. The ones who remembered my father were reluctant to talk about him; but after prodding them with questions, I learned that after he visited Jimmy and me at the Tewksbury almshouse on his way to Chicago, he had committed suicide.

What a poor, sorrowful soul my dad must have been at the end of his life. He was a total failure. He had gone to America with a beautiful wife and looked forward to a happy home with many children. Instead, he lost his wife and two children to death and put two of his children in the poorhouse! I actually found myself feeling pity for him. He had wanted so badly to do well in America. Being with the Irish people again, I vaguely recalled Dad's singing and the wonderful stories he told about Ireland and the faeries of Ireland. They had comforted me through many terrible times as a very young child. He probably knew they would. My hatred of him dissolved into love and pity. I was glad I had found his family.

We spent several weeks in beautiful Scotland, and Polly introduced us to her family. They were very gracious and hospitable. In our wanderings, we were lucky enough to see the Scottish crossbill seen only in Scotland and majestic golden eagles. Helen and Polly took long walks on the beach visiting the seals and numerous seabirds. I waited for them from a comfortable perch by the road. I heard the bark of the seals as they jockeyed for position among their large families and the excited call of the bickering seabirds. I heard no human voices. It was as though I had become the beach, the seals, and the birds. I took deep breaths of the salty sea air and let myself relax. How I loved Scotland.

We made a brief stop in rainy England before we returned home.

*   *   *

We resumed our regular schedule in Forest Hills. Polly and Helen continued work with the American Foundation for the Blind and lectured. Helen also focused on her books and articles for various newspapers and magazines. Thankfully, when Helen was home, she spent a great deal of her time in my company. It was comforting to just sit in the same room with her as she worked. I missed her so much when she was away. If she worked away from home, she eagerly hurried to my room at the end of the day to give me a full report of her activities and accomplishments and hear about my day. I tried very hard to sound happy and content when Helen was there, but I know she could sense my depression and unrest. What a pathetic old woman I had become.

*   *   *

In 1931 we had reason to celebrate. A year earlier, Helen had made an appearance before the U.S. Congress requesting libraries of Braille books for the blind. Congresswoman Ruth Baker Pratt and Congressman Reed Smoot presented the Pratt-Smoots Act which would provide $100,000 for Braille books for the blind. The bill was approved by Congress and signed by President Herbert Hoover on March 3, 1931. In April, at the World Council for the Blind, held in New York, Helen successfully pleaded with delegates from thirty-two nations to make Braille the standard alphabet for the blind throughout the world.

Another reason to celebrate the year 1931 was my award of an honorary degree from Temple University of Philadelphia and a fellowship from the Educational Institute of Scotland.

*   *   *

The following year the three of us celebrated with a trip to Concarneau, Brittany. Concarneau was a beautiful, quiet little fishing village located on the western tip of France overlooking the Atlantic Ocean. A medieval wall surrounded the little town conjuring all sorts of images of battles and other scenes played out hundreds of years earlier.

I spent many peaceful hours on the porch of our little hotel enjoying the fishy, salty smell of the ocean and listening to the waves wash noisily over the rocks and then retreat back to their source.

We were invited to be guests of Yugoslavian king Alexander, and Helen was asked to speak to leaders of the country about the rehabilitation of the blind. Our suite of rooms was rich and magnificent. We attended several extravagant parties while in Yugoslavia. It was a pleasant stay, and we enjoyed meeting Queen Maria and their three very rambunctious young sons. I always loved the luxury that surrounded us when we visited royalty or the very wealthy. Window and bed fabrics were beautifully woven and colorful. Soaps were scented, and towels were freshly aired and soft. Everything was spotless. Anything we requested was at our door almost immediately.

When we returned to our rooms in Concarneau, I was so exhausted and miserable that I was certain I would not live long. I wasn't even sure I would make it back to our home in Forest Hills. I obtained council in Brittany and prepared my last will and testament, making certain that Helen and Polly were well cared for. All of my pictures, written notes, and documents I had written about Helen and her education I bequeathed to our friend, author and publisher Nella Braddy Henney, with instructions that they should be used to assist Helen with her work.

*   *   *

I survived the trip back to Forest Hills, and we settled in for the long winter. Then in early December, Polly was rushed to the hospital for an appendicitis operation. She spent most of the month in the hospital. Helen also fell ill, and we were confined to our home for the entire winter. It was a dark and gloomy holiday season that year. I was feeling very old and depressed but did my best to cheerfully take care of Helen through her illness. The dark, dreary days seemed endless. It was a relief to get into my bed each night and escape the day through sleep.

By spring, everyone was feeling better. Polly rushed in one morning and told us she had seen the first spring flowers peeking up through the little drifts of snow that still lingered. Soon small soft buds peppered the limbs of the trees, and the scent of spring flowers filled the air. As always, the miraculous awakening of the earth to spring lifted my spirits. Helen and Polly bundled me up and guided me on long walks down our little street to admire the blessings of the season. I could hardly see but heard the birds that were busily gathering up twigs for their nests and excitedly discussing their building plans with their mates. When it was warm enough, we sat on the porch swing and talked about our plans for the summer.

*   *   *

It seemed impossible for me to travel again, but Helen and Polly convinced me to return with them to Scotland. Helen had been invited to speak for the commencement exercises at the University of Glasgow where she would receive an honorary degree of doctor of law. I couldn't miss such an important event, and I loved Scotland, so I agreed to go. We traveled to Scotland on a beautiful ship called the *President Harding*.

I was overwhelmed by Helen's speech on commencement day. She paid tribute to me. I could hardly control my emotions. I was so proud of what we had done. I loved her so much and was so thankful that I had been chosen to be her teacher and soul mate.

We were invited to the Educational Institute of Scotland where both Helen and I were presented with honorary fellowships. I usually wouldn't accept such an honor but felt compelled to do so this time. Helen was delighted, and I was pleased to have been recognized.

We visited London where Helen was introduced through Lady Astor to George Bernard Shaw. He was rough-edged, and we did not care for him very much. We were glad to continue our journey to Buckingham Palace and met King George and Queen Mary at a beautiful party on the grounds of the castle. Helen and I were asked to demonstrate how we communicated, and we were once again on the vaudeville stage. We didn't mind performing for this wonderful, kind king and queen.

*   *   *

I could not continue the pace any longer, and we rented a little Elizabethan cottage in Kent for the remainder of the summer. It was called Memory Cottage, and we certainly would remember it. It was dark, gloomy, and much too small for the three of us. The weather was damp, and I soon was ill with bronchitis.

We returned to Scotland for better weather and lived in a little cottage in Hannafore, West Looe, owned by a friend of Polly's. It was on the edge of a cliff. The hillsides behind it were covered with forget-me-nots and primrose. Their heavy scent and the fresh air revitalized me, and my health improved a great deal. We all loved Scotland and were delighted to be back there again.

By August I was much stronger. One sunny, warm day, I was lounging peacefully on the porch when a young man rode his bicycle to our door to deliver a telegram. John Macy had died of a heart attack in a hospital in Pennsylvania. I was stunned. It was a message I never expected to hear.

My darling John was dead. He was only fifty-five years old and apparently lived in poverty. Helen was very upset and mourned the loss of her working companion and friend. Helen and I both agreed we would pay for his funeral and burial.

We spent our last week in Scotland with Lord and Lady Aberdeen whom we had known for several years. We came back to the United States with a new little friend they gave us, a Shetland collie named Dileas. I was delighted to have another dog in the house.

28

LAST LIGHT

My health began failing rapidly in 1935. I was quite frail. The sight in my left eye was nearly gone and pained me unmercifully. I had severe stomach distress and suffered from skin boils. I was hospitalized for a short time, and it was determined that I was suffering from heart disease. Sometimes I was confused and regularly forgot what I was thinking or talking about in the middle of a sentence.

Helen and Polly convinced me to take another vacation in the Catskills knowing how much I loved it there. I did love the Catskills. I couldn't see the beauty anymore, but the warmth of the sun, the sounds, and the scents were there, and I could remember how everything looked.

However, while in the Catskills, I couldn't get the warm, beautiful tropics out of my mind. Our trip to Puerto Rico had been so special and so healing, and I yearned to go again. I must have shared my feelings with Helen and Polly because they arranged for us to leave the Catskills and go to Jamaica.

Jamaica of course was beautiful. The temperature hovered around eighty-two degrees during our stay, and the countryside was thick with greenery and colorful flowers. Now, neither Helen nor I could see them, so Polly fingerspelled to Helen and told me about the beautiful scenes that surrounded us. I could picture the palms and bamboo that shaded every little lane, and I once again enjoyed fresh bananas picked right off the tree! Everything felt and smelled wonderful.

I sat in the warmth of the sun on our little porch with Helen while Polly went on walks. She brought us flowers of every color and shape imaginable that she found. I felt the shapes of each flower and enjoyed their wonderful scents. Helen never left my side.

Since I could not see and suffered from so many ailments, I did not enjoy Jamaica like I had Puerto Rico. My body was so worn and tired I could have easily just stayed in bed. But I managed to get up in the mornings and dress and was glad I did. Helen, Polly, and I enjoyed each other's company so much, and we all enjoyed experiencing Jamaica.

Soon August arrived, and we returned to our home in Forest Hills. The heat was unbearable, so we escaped to a little cottage by the ocean in Greenport, Long Island. It was much cooler there, and I was glad to settle into a quiet routine again.

*   *   *

In April 1936, I had my left eye operated on in an effort to restore some of my vision. When the bandages were removed, I found that I could see much better. A few weeks later, I awoke to excruciating pain in my eye. The surgery had failed. The only way to relieve the pain was to remove my eye. I was totally blind.

Oh, how I hated the return to darkness! It was something I had feared for over fifty years, since I was blind as a child.

The heat of summer was soon upon us, and we escaped to a cottage by the ocean in Peconic Bay on Eastern Long Island. I rallied somewhat and even attempted to wade in the water. But I had been in bed and inactive for so long that I found myself getting dizzy and had to be rescued by Polly and Helen. My dizziness and severe weakness did not subside, and I was taken to the hospital where I was told there was a blood clot that had interfered with the flow of blood to my heart. There was nothing they could do, and I was taken back to Forest Hills by ambulance. How I hated old age! My body was so old and tired; and yet my soul, the inner me, felt like it had felt forever, all energy. How strange is this human life.

Helen and Polly were wonderful nurses. I was in my bed a good part of the day, but in the evenings they helped me to the table for dinner, and we sat companionably in our beautiful little living room in the evenings. Close friends and neighbors sometimes visited. I didn't take part in the conversations very much but enjoyed listening to them. Helen was always chattering away in my hand. I cherished this time with the two people I loved best in the world. I knew I wouldn't be with them long and wanted to enjoy every moment we were together.

29

FAREWELL

I am not thinking clearly. Sometimes I awake in the Tewksbury almshouse and have breakfast in Forest Hills. Then my mind wanders again to perhaps Scotland or maybe vague glimpses and memories of my beloved brother, Jimmy. I find myself talking to him. I hear my dad singing my favorite Irish songs and then again am at my desk at Perkins. I feel the warmth of John's arms around me and hear him whisper, "I love you," in my ear. I feel my mother and sister Nellie's presence and know we will soon be reunited.

Then I am awakened to the present from the feel of Helen's warm, soft hand as she speaks to me gently, telling me of her love for me and appreciation for removing her veil of darkness. She spends hours by my bedside reminding me of all of our wonderful adventures. And then again she tells me she loves me. Polly is also often there. I love the sound of her voice, with the Scottish brogue. It is comforting, and how I will miss it!

I know Polly can take care of Helen. Helen will be fine. She will get over my death as we all get over death and continue on with her life's work. I am so proud of her. And I know she will think of me. Our souls are much too intertwined to be separated by the death of my human form.

Farewell, my darling Helen.

Epilogue

Anne Sullivan Macy died at seven-thirty in the morning on October 20, 1936, with Helen Keller by her side holding her hand. She was seventy years old. Helen Keller was fifty-six. They had been together for fifty years. Anne's ashes were placed in the National Cathedral in Washington, D.C.

Selected Bibliography

Books:

Braddy, Nelle (Henney). *Anne Sullivan Macy: The Story Behind Helen Keller.* Garden City, NY: Doubleday, Doran, 1933.

French, Kimberly. *Perkins School for the Blind.* Charleston, South Carolina: Arcadia Publishing, 2004.

Herrman, Dorothy. *Helen Keller: A Life.* Chicago, Illinois: University of Chicago Press, 1998.

Keller, Helen. *The Story of My Life.* New York, NY: Bantam Books, 1990. *Teacher: Anne Sullivan Macy.* Garden City, New York: Doubleday & Company 1956.

Lash, Joseph P. *Helen and Teacher.* Redding, Massachusetts: Addison-Wesley Publishing Company 1980.

Taylor, Jean Welt. *Gentle Hand to Victory.* Xlibris Corporation, 2004.

Articles:

"The New Outlook for the Blind." M. Robert Barnett, editor. 1966.

"The Liberator of Helen Keller." P. W. Wilson. 1933.

"Annie Mansfield Sullivan Macy, Helen Keller's 'Teacher.'" Alison Bergmann. 1996.

"Pencil Writing." Perkins Institute for the Blind library excerpt from talk given to Harvard class at Perkins in 1951.

Internet:

Massachusetts Poorhouse History. "Historical Overview of the American Poorhouse System—History of the 19th Century American Poorhouses *http://www.poorhousestory.com/history.htm*

Social History of the State Hospital System in Massachusetts. "Mass. State Hospitals: Social History". *http://1856.org/socialhistory.html*

Tewksbury Historical Society, Tewksbury Massachusetts. "State Hospital (Tewksbury Almshouse)", "Tewksbury State Hospital Register of Historic Places with the United States Department of the Interior", "100th Anniversary of the Tewksbury State Hospital held on October 13, 1954", 1883 edition of Puck Magazine "The Whitewash is Too Thin" courtesy of Michael Kelley, Deocratic Response Supporting Governor Benjamin Butler and The Tewksbury Investigation Committee of 1883, Boston Advertiser on May 7, 1883, "Tewksbury Investigation", Lowell Sun Weekly newspaper articles concerning Tewksbury Investigation. *http://www.tewksburyhistoricalsociety.org*

American Foundation for the Blind. "Anne Sullivan Macy: Miracle Worker" *http://www.afb.org/annesullivan*

American Foundation for the Blind. "Letters to Helen Keller from Anne Sullivan Macy", "Wright Humason School", "Final Years and Legacy", "Helen Keller Archives", "Talking Books" *http://www.afb.org*

Association Review, "John Hitz Honored" by Frank W. Booth, editor, *http://books.google.com*

Wikipedia, Forest Hills, New York, "Forest Hills, Queens" *http://en.wikipedia.org*

Massachusetts Wildflowers. Glen Corbiere "Flowers of Massachusetts". *http://www.dragonhunter.net/flowers.html*

Massachusetts Fauna. "Massachusetts—Flora and fauna" *http://www.city/states/Massachusetts-Flora-and-fauna.html*

Feeding Hills, Massachusetts. Feeding Hills Community Profile. "Feeding Hills, Massachusetts". *http://www.epodunk.com*

McCorkell Line Passanger Ships 1778-1897. "McCorkell Line" *http://www.mccorkelline.com*

Miller Center of Public Affairs. University of Virginia. Gerald Baliles, editor. "Ulysses S. Grant", "Rutherford B. Hayes". *http://millercenter.org*

Washington, DC, A National Register of Historic Places Travel Itinerary. "Volta Labortatory and Bureau". "Dr. Alexander Graham Bell". *http://www.nps.gov/nr/travel/wash/dc14.htm*

Virtualology. "Alexander Graham Bell". *http://www.alexandergrahambell.org/*

New York Times Archives. "Puck on Wheels", "Investigating at Tewksbury", "The Situation at Tewksbury", "State Wards", "About Tewksbury", "The Almshouse". *http://query.nytimes.com*

Perkins School for the Blind. Perkins Museum. "Founders", "Laura Bridgman", "Helen Keller", "History". *http://www.perkinsmuseum.org*

Puerto Rico. Weather, trees and wildlife. *http://www.gotopuertorico.com/*

Netstate. Massachusetts. "Massachusetts Economy", "Geography". *http://www.netstate.com*

Center for Lowell History—University of Massachusetts. "Tewksbury Almshouse". *http://library.umi.edu*

The Official Website of the City of Tuscumbia, Alabama. *http://www.cityoftuscumbia.org*

Scotland. *http://visitscotland.com*

Western France Tourist Board. "Brittany". *http://westernfrancetouristboard.com*

Wikipedia Enclyclopedia. "Civil War", "Radcliffe College", "Dr. Alexander Graham Bell", "Samuel Clemens", "Wright-Hamuson School for the Deaf", "Civil Rights Act", "Tobacco Blight", "Edward Hale", "Ruth Baker Pratt", "Congressman Reed". *http://www.wikipedia.org*

Wrentham, Massachusetts Community Profile. MA HomeTownLocator. *http://massachusetts.hometownlocator.com/MA/Norfolk/Wrentham. cfm*

Made in the USA
Middletown, DE
15 February 2017